Romance Your Writer Within

And Reawaken Your Passion to Write

by

Melba Burns, Ph.D.

Romance Your Writer Within
& Reawaken Your Passion To Write
Published by Soul Writes Books
May 2011

All rights reserved.
Copyright © 2010 by Melba Burns

Cover design by Eve Lees
Interior book design by Roxane Leigh

No part of this book may be reproduced or transmitted in any form or by any means electronic or mechanical, including photocopying, recording, or by any information storage and retrieval system without permission in writing from the copyright holder.

Melba Burns
219-633 Bucket Wheel Place
Vancouver, British Columbia.
Canada V5Z 4A7

ISBN 978-0-9689439-1-5

Romance Your Writer Within

And Reawaken Your Passion to Write

Melba Burns, Ph.D.

Published by Soul Writes Books
Vancouver, B. C.
Canada

To my Mother, Mabel Richardson,
Who always said,
"We're late bloomers in this family."

Contents

Introduction.. Page v
1. Invite A Conversation... 1
2. Prepare To Receive Her... 6
3. Woo Her Voice Back 8
4. Gaze Into Her Eyes... 14
5. Buy Her Flowers 16
6. Ask Her 4 Important Questions................................ 18
7. Don't Judge: Accept Her 23
8. Call Her By Name 27
9. Understand Her Creative Proces 31
10. Make Time To Meditate 38
11. Speak Truth 41
12. Have Courage To Express The Pain 45
13. Write Love Letters.. 47
14. Ask: What Truly Has Meaning?................................ 50
15. Say "Yes" More Than "No" 54
16. Reject Rejection 56
17. Appreciate Her 59
18. Lovingly Reward Her.. 63
19. Feel Your Feelings... 66
20. See The Wide-Eyed Child In Her............................. 69
21. Rewrite History 72
22. Examine Your Resistance.. 75
23. Release Self-Sabotage 84
24. Make Peace With Other Pieces 88

25. Love That Former Self	90
26. Forgive	93
27. Dream Big And Clarify Your Goals	99
28. Share Your Stories	102
29. Treasure Map	107
30. Continue To Hear Her Stories	110
31. Truly See Her	113
32. Remember, She Is Your friend	118
33. Play And Have Fun	121
34. Make Time For Her	125
35. Commit	129
36. Be Gentle With Her	134
37. Take Her Into Your Bed	136
38. Be Nice to Her in the Morning	138
39. Give Her Permission To Be Naughty	141
40. Encourage Her Sensuality	144
41. Keep The Sparks Lit	150
42. Ask: What Opens Your Heart Wider?	156
43. Remember Miracles	161
44. Take Her to a Writer's Circle	167
45. Show How You Believe in Her	172
46. Converse With Her	176
47. Ask For Her Help	180
48. Make It A Habit to Romance Her	184
49. Commune With Her	191
50. Give Thanks For Your Loving Relationship	197
Acknowledgements	203

Introduction

Here you are in midlife, sharp, alert – and still dreaming! Poised however, between conflicting feelings of self-doubt and determination, fear and excitement, you're chafing at the bit because there's so much you want to do, and you wonder if it is possible. One of your dreams may be to write a novel, or a book of short stories or essays, maybe a memoir, but you ask yourself: Is this realistic? After all, you are ultra busy, life is moving fast, so how could you fit it in? Besides, the thought of writing is a tiny bit terrifying, and when you ponder it, you're not sure you feel the same passion about creativity that you once did, a few years ago.

Well, as you learn to Romance your Writer Within, to court, honor, respect, and love your inner Creative Self like you would a lover, you can reawaken a beautiful sleeping goddess, your Writer Within, and she will help you to write.

Introduction

As we women age, we deal with all kinds of issues like hot flashes, new wrinkles, physical challenges – our bodies don't behave or look like they did twenty years ago - so we often fall into self-doubt and lose confidence in our abilities. Then, if we forget a word or someone's name, we fear that our brain must have changed, and our cognitive clarity diminished. Suddenly, we wonder: Who am I? What is my identity now? Am I as invisible as I sometimes feel? What about my dreams? Dare I even dream them anymore?

Diane Vilas, an essay-writer in a book called *Our Turn, Our Time*, asked another significant question regarding our bodily changes: "What if there's a spiritual purpose behind this shift in body chemistry?... a spiritual milestone with the potential for transformation, transcendence, even evolution..."[1] Ms. Vilas found, through research, and studying her own menopausal process for ten years that as one's estrogen diminishes the right hemisphere of the brain "becomes more active. We access more of our creativity; our aesthetic sense, our intuition."[2] So, if you once dreamed you would express yourself creatively in some form, there is hope!

Dr. Daniel Amen, founder of the Amen Brain Clinics (with locations currently in four American cities, they have performed well over 30,000 brain scans), absolutely believes there is hope. He knows first-hand that a human brain can change. In his fascinating book, *Making a Good Brain Great*, he states that "In stunning new research ... investigators demonstrated that adult human brains generate new cells after all." [3] He adds that we can indeed make our brains better: "The great news is that the brain is malleable and able to change... You can make a good brain great." [4]

So, no matter what is going on with you now in midlife or later, scientific evidence indicates that it is never too late to do what you want – like write. You were born with creative abilities and you still have them. Just as you can expand the neurological pathways in your brains, you can reawaken your passion to write.

Do you remember when you were courting a lover? Or he/she was courting you? Romance was in the air and it lifted your spirits up so the whole world looked rosy. Well, whether you wish to court a new lover, or whether you wish to live alone for the rest of your life, you can still court your Writer Within. All you have to do is to remember the principles for interpersonal communication in your relationships and apply them *intra*personally – to your Creative Self.

Researchers Brewi and Brennan assert: "The conversion of mid-life demands that the inner world become as real to us as the outer world. The second half of life is a journey inward and it is from our own inner experience that we slowly learn to discern our own genuine values." [5]

This book will show you how to romance your Writer Within. It will lead you through the tentative steps, past your self-doubts, past any resistance you have to putting words to paper, so you actually learn to not only like your inner Creative Self, but to love her.

Step by step, you can romance your Writer Within, engage with her and get to know her, eventually commit, commune with and partner with her so you don't feel so alone in this creative process; so you are confident that you have an inner Writer to work with. Through this process, you will reawaken your passion to write, reclaim your dreams and your power, and once again remember who you are. Watch out, you will probably be writing till you're 100!

What is The Writer Within?

* It is the essence of your Self that you often ignore, deny, run from, or keep too busy for.

* It is that inner feminine aspect – which we'll refer to in the feminine as "she" or "her." She is your Creative Self.

* It is a divine connection to Source; your own uniqueness.

* It is that deep knowingness that doesn't question how it knows; it just knows.

* Your Writer Within guides your pen onto pristine pages and writes words that fill you with surprise and delight.

* In the night, when all is dark and the silence is too severe and you're alone, it is a sweet breath breathed upon your face. You wonder, but do not question where it came from.

* It isn't out there, in movies, in your child's eyes or your lover's arms, but in you. It is that gift within.

* It is mysterious - but known.

* It is love.

We speak about how "green" our lives must be to sustain our planet, but what about "greening" our very selves? Creativity is our life force, and if we do not honor it, if we choose to ignore it, our very human existence threatens to become unsustainable. We squeeze off our potential so many possibilities dwindle away. Haven't you heard yourself say: "I don't have the time; I'm too busy; I just can't fit it into my hectic schedule?" So what then? It begins to die off: your *greatness* – and you forget who you were born to be.

At midlife, you may indeed forget how sure of yourself you once were; you may feel intensely challenged, off-balance, deeply grieving some of your losses; including your former identity. You may not only see new wrinkles on your face, but feel your vital energy dimming; you may fall into the old belief that chronology dictates how you should be for your age, that is, you must be getting old. Not true. Your attitude to life is a choice, and you can choose to move ahead and express who you truly are.

Transitional discomfort and confusion at midlife can crack you open to an inner dimension that you may not have been ready for before this time. This was something I experienced when my mother died; my heart seemed to crack open. But through exploring the depths of those lonely places, those inner caverns of the new midlife orphan, I was able to venture into myself in deeper, more honest ways, and heal. How? By putting pen to paper, I made my way through those painful feelings and reclaimed a closer relationship with my inner Self. By writing your way through your own feelings, you can too.

As Dr. Gene D. Cohen says in his book *The Creative Age*: "Midlife is a powerful time for the expression of human potential because it combines the capacity for insightful reflection with a powerful desire to create meaning in life." [6]

This book will guide you to see and embrace more of your self, to create meaning in your life and by taking conscious steps, to renew your relationship with your Creative Self. You will forge through blocks, old beliefs, fears and resistance, to restore your creativity – and reawaken your passion to write.

Through writing and communication with your Creative Self – also known as Writer Within – you will re-engage with your creativity, which Sir Ken Robinson terms "the most powerful capacity that we have." [7]

Whether you have been married to your writing for twenty years, have been engaged for a little while, or are just beginning to court your inner Writer, this book will restore and empower your relationship with your Writer Within.

If you want to reawaken your passion to write, work with the exercises in this book:

* You will reconnect with your Source and learn to write more fluidly; in alignment with your Writer Within, you will know this highest aspect of yourself. Open it at any page and you'll be reminded to keep the lines of communication open to Writer Within so you can work together.

* Together with your Creative Self, you will explore the process of getting words onto the pages; poems, song lyrics, stories, essays, non-fiction or novels written.

* When you're feeling frustrated, this book will remind you why you want to write – and will guide you back to putting your pen on the paper.

* Energizing exercises and the author's deeply personal stories will assist you to release old blocks to your creativity. You will examine and let go of self-sabotage, which may have been a constant companion for years, so your writing will flow easily.

* You'll learn how to persist when you feel like giving up.

* This book will remind you that the only way you can fail is to quit, so to keep on offering up your heart to your creativity. In doing so, you'll learn to love yourself more after reading and participating in the 50 chapters.

* You will restore your belief in yourself as a creative being, your self-esteem will rise, and you will no longer feel alone as you write.

* This book will remind you that you were born creative, so you'll begin to remember who you really are. Old wrinkles of self-doubt will fade away and you will learn to write with wonder and passion.

As a writer for the past 40 years, and a creative writing instructor for 20, the exercises contained herein have helped me and hundreds of other people to do what this book will inspire you to do: Romance Your Writer Within – and Reawaken your Passion to Write.

How Do You Romance Your Writer Within?

Most of us know what it's like to be romanced or courted by a lover, or, we have done the courting ourselves, right? So, having a loving intrapersonal relationship with your Creative Self/Writer Within requires most of the same caring qualities as those in an interpersonal relationship with your lover. You have to snuggle up to your Inner Self in similar ways as you would snuggle up to your lover. Love your Writer Within as you would love your partner.

Just as certain gestures deepen your interpersonal connection with your lover, so do loving thoughts and actions awaken your intrapersonal communication with your Writer Within. Often referred to as the inner "feminine," the being aspect rather than the doing, "she" is imaginative, deep and wise, and when you learn to open to "her" you expand your creativity.

Remember, your Writer Within wants you too. As Rumi reminds us...

"No lover wants union with the Beloved without the Beloved also wanting the lover." [8]

This book will help you to reawaken loving and honest communication with your Beloved Writer Within. So you get to know her and truly engage with her. So you develop a loving, passionate, sustainable partnership, and merge. So you become prolific with your creative babies that thrive and grow and contribute to the world. Also... as we work with the metaphor of romance you may even learn ways to breathe new life into the relationship with your lover.

Remember, you were born creative, and all you need do is awaken it. Sir Ken Robinson, who was knighted for his work in the field of creativity, says, "Everyone is born with tremendous capacities for creativity. The trick is to develop these capacities" [9]

Your creativity can lead you to places you've hardly ever been – but places that feel familiar. As a child you knew it and trusted it, until some adult or teacher convinced you that you weren't an artist. So you made a decision: "Why would I even attempt to write?" The adults made a mistake about you. Perhaps they had given up on their own creativity, or tucked their inner artist away; packed her up with the junk in the attic. You can romance her back. She is still there, inside you. But you must pursue her – as you would a lover. You must learn to treat her as you would your most beloved relationship. This book will help you to do just that. Exciting, isn't it? Let's begin…

Chapter 1. Invite A Conversation

When you meet a person you're attracted to, you usually ask questions so they may start to open up. To develop a relationship with this person, you must listen to what they are saying – otherwise, they will sense your insincerity, close the door to their heart and turn away.

It is the same principle for romancing your Writer Within: Ask good questions, then listen to what she says.

The question "Why" is a crucial one because if you don't know your motivation to write, you probably won't get very far. But if you know why, you will create a strong foundation for putting pen to paper.

When I was a young woman of 25, I wrote in my journal: I want to write because I want to become a very wise woman and share that wisdom with others. I still refer to that entry when I resist my writing. In times of resistance, rejection, or self-doubt, you too can return to your responses to this question; they will fortify you and renew your passion to write.

Ask "why write?" & then listen:

Some of your answers might sound like this...

* I WANT TO WRITE to tell my stories.

* To inspire others, so they know they can make changes.

* To allow the crazy-wild-me to flop onto the page in whatever form it takes.

* To find out what really is inside me.

* To have people read my work and, hopefully, enjoy it; laugh, cry, feel what is inside of them and be touched.

* To make a contribution to this world.

* To enjoy exploring other people's lives in my characters.

* To inspire readers, touch hearts and open them to remember who they are.

* To go on inner journeys blindly, not knowing where.

* To appreciate what's around me and express it in poetry.

* To trust that what I have to say means something.

* To write from any mood, any time, anywhere; honoring my soul.

* To tell my stories, so others get a sense of transcending their own challenges; that by writing, they can learn from their own.

* To enliven myself - and to empower others.

* To assist my soul's transformation – touch another soul.

* To speak through loved ones I've known; give them voice, and learn to understand them better.

* To gain entry to portals of deep wisdom and knowledge.

* To lift off from *mundane* and rediscover the poetic realm.

* To say a holy YES to life and try to be my best self.

* To make some money - hey, what a novel thought!

* I want to write because I must.

...acknowledge to yourself whether you would have to die if it were denied you to write. This above all – ask yourself in the stillest hour of the night: must I write? And if this should be affirmative...then build your life according to this necessity;...
Rainer Maria Rilke [10]

Why Write?

*To welcome back the magic you've forgotten – to let the doves fly out
Of the hat. You write to give birth to a brand new character,
To be inside another person's skin; to know that person
Intimately as they appear all shiny and wet on the page.*

*You write to see the person you keep hidden. To greet her and say,
"I know you're in there, welcome." You write to put a poultice on
Your pain and pull it to the surface – to lance it with your pen.*

*You write to free the beast, to let her roar with unrequited passion
And devour raw the meat of ancient dreams.
You write because in times of deepest anguish, of highest joy
You try to capture it. In times of solitude, you simply must.*

*You write to know more about yourself, that amazing person
Who can't even say it to your mirror, the one yearning to speak
Out from her soul. So you open up to that place inside; exploring
With gentle probes, like a lover. You write to mark up a clean
white page with delight and the scent of yourself.*

*In this writing, you may touch another who needs to hear those words.
Who needs to be reminded that his words, her stories, also matter;
We're all human and we all want to know we're not alone here.
You write because it's important, because you want to express;
In doing so, you remember who you are.*

*When you write, the guardians of your soul whisper their names.
Bow before you like elders in a sacred ceremony, chanting Namaste.
So, you offer your thoughts up to the divine, and indeed remember –
Deep inside you, buried so deep you often can't find it, deep inside
is a spark, and by blowing it onto the page, it ignites and illuminates
your own Greatness.*

Now write out your own responses to: Why Write?

Chapter 2. Prepare To Receive Her

When that special person in our lives comes to visit, we clean up our homes – don't we? We dust, vacuum, fluff up the pillows on the couch – and sometimes, we even light candles. So, clean up your office, remove the clutter – and act as if a very special person is coming over.

Your Writer Within is special. She will feel more comfortable if the desk is tidied and polished, and if there is a sense of order. Your writing will feel more meaningful.

If you live in clutter, how can you see the beauty of anything around? You can't, it's covered with junk. But if you are prepared to welcome this treasured being in a more loving manner, then the words may flow more freely. Your Writer Within will feel received with joy.

Clean up your writing area so it reflects these values and watch your writing improve.

Another way to prepare is to purchase little pocket-sized notebooks, and carry them everywhere. When you're out for a walk and hear a great phrase, or receive an idea for an essay or a short story, you can jot it down. Without that notebook, brilliant ideas or lyrics would be forgotten. Besides, when you're out of your own home, that's a time when your mind is often more freed up and the ideas flow. Try it. It works.

At night, dreams and great ideas dance jigs in your head, so make sure you have your notebook and pen beside the bed. If you believe you're going to remember your dream when you awaken, forget that; it will have slipped into the ethers. So write it down when it happens. Or write whatever compels you to put pen to paper.

Often I get insomnia, and may not realize what is tossing around in my mind, but once I've turned on the light and scrawled some notes to myself, albeit in a sleepy state, I can usually sink into slumber.

As you prepare to receive from your Writer Within, you will face your writing with a sense of excitement and amazement, for are you not privileged to be able to express on paper what is within your soul? You know you are. And your midlife Self is reawakening to a fuller life.

Chapter 3. Woo Her Voice Back

In relationships, you encourage your loved ones to express their deepest thoughts, and this usually helps the relationship to grow. But what about you? Are you able to express certain thoughts that may feel unacceptable to you?

Writer Within wants you to express your voice.

In the beginning was the word. You may not remember that yowl as a newborn, that first raw bawl from the slimy upside-down infant that was you, still attached to the umbilical chord. Mother is still sweaty from her hours of exertion, from times she thought she might die, so great was her pain – but here you are, howling infant, strange looking, still covered in the white-capped swill of pushing into the world.

Traumatic, yes! That pushing is the strongest you may ever do – like moving a 50-ton boulder out of the way;

or, like swimming upstream, leaping against gravity and the elements – all for Birth. To be here! That life force, compelling. You'll do anything for that emergence into life! You've been nine months gestating for that celebration into this world, and now, you must express your very existence, wailing and squalling..."Hey, I'm here everybody! Aren't you glad to see me?"

But, then what happens?

Through the resounding battles of childhood you learn to hold back, and any cry you make is shushed up: "Shush," when you whimper in the night. "Shush... there, there, don't cry."

So you learned that coos and laughter were welcome here – but not the other sounds, not whimpers and sniffles. Sometimes, they were greeted with, "Here, I'll give you something to cry about." The heavy hand was applied to your already heavy heart; once again you shushed up.

In school, in mechanical rows of other children, you were admonished, "Be quiet. Don't speak unless you raise your hand." So, you buttoned up once more, and the pain of anything you wanted to express was tucked away behind your glistening eyes, like a key glittering at the bottom of a deep pool.

There were probably secrets you stuffed away, the ones you were forbidden to tell: collusions, family things: How Mom and Dad fought too much. How you feared that your family wasn't like those of your friends. Other things too: you tried to tell, but soon realized it was better to "shush up."

Keep quiet. Shut the door to pain. Bolt it so nobody could ever enter -mostly, so your words could not get out. So, there they stay, locked in and festering, just under the surface.

Why?

Why, because you're loyal to friends and family. So loyal, you've chosen them over your own life. Besides, if you expressed your truth, you believed that you wouldn't be loved anymore; like some tribes do, that you would be castigated for exposing the clan's secrets. So, you chose the group over your own soul – and died a little as this beloved family showed you what you believed to be love. You conformed, sold out your soul and your creativity. One more voice silenced.

Haven't you heard yourself stay silent when you really shouldn't have? How about the time when you wanted to shout, "Stop that racist joke!" Or counter some other slur? As you've grown older, you may have learned to speak up for those ills, but what about speaking up for yourself?

That's the hardest thing to do. The critic is loud, it voices all the reasons you should remain civilized and silent. So, you need to tell it, "Thanks for sharing, but I'll let you criticize later."

How then do you regain your natural voice?

By writing it.

Write, write and write – without any kind of judgment whatsoever; simply witness what comes out. You don't have to approve of it – just accept that voice for whatever it wants to say. Give yourself permission to write the worst junk in the world, and say, "Today, this stuff wanted to come out, and that's okay."

Try it. Recapture your voice. Romance your voice back and let her say things. Oh, you might not like some of it. But other things your voice says might be important truths you've been trying to stuff down for years. Like the following…

* I hate my job, so why am I working there?

* Maybe this 10-year relationship isn't worth saving.

* Maybe I should see a doctor for this symptom I'm having.

* Yikes, what do I do now that I'm aware of these things?

* I don't like living in this apartment, it doesn't suit me.

* I'm attracted to that man I see every day in the elevator, so now what?

* I feel happy when I'm putting words down on paper.

* I remember that my eighth-grade teacher used to praise me for my compositions, so maybe I had the gift? Oh, how bold to say that. Well, I enjoy writing this. Is it possible that I really am creative? Maybe!

In expressing your truth, you will find that you have even more to say, and your Writer Within will feel like you want to hear her. You'll inspire others too.

A few years ago, I took a songwriting course, to find my voice in singing. Here I was in my early fifties and I'd never sung solos. Well, in four months, I was singing solos to 250 people – singing my own songs and loving it! Thrilled that I was finding what was in me.

I was singing about the hard stuff, too, such as a song about my son, *"Where'd it go so wrong?"* I had to be willing to dive into that pain. The first time I sang it to the group, the song was nearly inaudible through my own tears. But I kept on going; sang it anyway – heard my own voice. Later, one fellow said that he'd never cried over a song, and with tears in his eyes, shared with me how this song "got to him."

Oh, isn't that what we want? To move someone to his/her own feelings; to know that our voice has so touched another that there's been a deep soul connection? That's what one voice can do: connect us with others. As we express our voice we give our love. Isn't that what we are all about, giving our talents and expressing who we are?

Let your voice be heard. Hear it yourself. Listen. Come out. Squall like the newborn and yowl your life onto pages, onto airwaves, into your friends' lives and into the hearts of your family.

When you let your voice come out and be heard, you will find it and learn to trust it – to expand the being that you are. Your Writer Within will sing along in delight with you, to a passionate tune.

Chapter 4. Gaze Into Her Eyes

No, I'm not kidding. Remember, lovers gaze into each other's eyes, and feel their relationship intensify. Writers need to do this too – to start falling in love with your Writer Within. When you do, you'll see the loving qualities you have within yourself and how much more you have to contribute.

Gaze into the mirror and affirm that you're willing to have a great relationship with your Writer Within. Gazing into one's own eyes is a recognized spiritual exercise that has helped many people to get back in touch with themselves.

When I first really looked into my eyes in the mirror, I did feel weird at first. But then as I really focused deeply, I saw something different; as if my soul were communicating with me. It seemed as if my Inner Self, my Writer Within, was saying:

I am so pleased that you are opening up to me. I want you to see who guides you, who will always be here for you; a voice of Love from your heart. Oh, please keep tuning into me and let us live together.

It brought tears, which was a little scary, but it changed me. I was very grateful for that strong suggestion to do this. I hope you try it. You will start to honor yourself more and begin to accept more of your own writing – without criticizing it.

As Julia Cameron states in her classic book for recovering creative beings: "Art lies in the moment of encounter: we meet our truth and we meet ourselves; we meet ourselves and we meet our self-expression." [11]

Gaze into yourself, meet your truth and your buried passion will peek out from behind the masks, the pretense of trying to control who you think you are – so you become your true Self.

Chapter 5. Buy Her Flowers

Don't you love receiving flowers from a loved one? Yesterday, a friend gave me a dozen beautiful roses – and that act made my day. In any relationship, the gift of flowers speaks love, and will lift your energy.

BE the one who demonstrates love by investing $5.00 in flowers for your desk, or your coffee table. It will make your writing area more sacred. Those flowers could also make you aware of the beauty in your life, and open you to more of it.

The poet and acclaimed American writer, May Sarton, writes of flowers in her moving book, *Journal of a Solitude*: "When I am alone the flowers are... felt as presences. Without them I would die.... They live and die in a few days; they keep me closely in touch with process, with growth... I am floated in their moments." [12]

As you gaze at the soft, strong, smooth petal of that yellow tulip or red rose or purple iris, contemplate it as a reflection of your innermost self: If those delicate-looking flowers can withstand rains and storms, whatever the season may throw at them, you can too.

At midlife, you may be grieving losses that are common at this stage of your life. So, it is doubly important to see and value your own Inner Self. Go out today and buy yourself a bouquet of flowers, to reflect back your own inner love and beauty.

Yes, you have your own inner beauty, whether you acknowledge that or not: it is your Writer Within who is constantly with you. Let that beauty flow onto pages and into your stories and novels. You will stir your passion and reawaken your dreams.

"It's my contention that the mere presence of passion within you —and the enthusiasm that comes with it — is all you need to fulfill your dreams."
Wayne Dyer [13]

Chapter 6. Ask Important Questions

To romance your honey, wouldn't you ask about who they are and what they want in life? Then you need to listen carefully, for how else would you get to truly know that person?

As you sit at your desk about to write, sometimes words don't come. What do you do? If you ask yourself the following four questions, write out the answers, read them over and listen, you will move your writing forward.

(a) **Why do I WANT to write this piece?**

(b) **Why SHOULDN'T I write this piece?**

(c) **What if I DON'T write this piece?**

(d) **Why MUST I write this?**

(a) **Why do I WANT to write this?**

Romance your Writer Within and ask her all the reasons why you *THINK* you want to do this. *For example: I think this might touch people. I have a good idea here and I really like the topic. I want to explore this piece and see where it goes. I'd like to write my mother's story. I'd like to write about how it feels to be a midlife orphan, etc.*

(b) **Why SHOULDN'T I write this?**

Let the critic have a heyday. *This will never go out into the world anyway... Who do you think you are? You have no talent. I will be too emotional to write some of these things... You're a phony and you know it. Mom always said you were too big for your britches...* Get the idea? Just put down all the negative stuff you can think of.

In beginning a relationship (yes, even if you're over fifty or sixty) you can give your *intended* lover the opportunity to say why he or she shouldn't be with you. Once these old thoughts and fears are shared, they seem to pop like bubbles into thin air. Then, there's more space for the real truth to develop and more depth for your relationship to evolve.

In developing a relationship with your Writer Within, it also helps to get out all the negative stuff as it clears the path for deeper communication.

(c) What if I DON'T write this?

If you have something to express, but don't, then you SUPPRESS it.

Often, this goes even deeper; you forget it entirely and REPRESS IT.

Then, you wonder why you get DEPRESSED. Through my own life and the lives of students I've worked with for over the past twenty years, I know it is healing to EXPRESS what's really going on. Even if the topic is really yucky or difficult, write it anyway. You don't have to show it to anybody, just get it out. You'll feel better.

Ask: **What if I don't write this piece I'm pondering?**

* I might be depriving myself and others of something really good.

* This piece will stay stuck inside me, never to be born.

* This piece deserves to be written.

* The story of my mother's life won't be written.

* Others might want to know about being a midlife orphan.

* I would be mad at myself for letting myself down.

* It would be very sad if it weren't written.

If you suppress it, you might end up seriously depressed. Isn't it better if you just EXPRESS whatever is going on?

With your Beloved, or within any relationship, if you nurse your grudges and don't express them, tension and anger builds up in your body and the situation worsens. If you continue to avoid true communication you risk ruining that relationship. But you can save it, even enhance it, by expressing your truth.

Romance your Writer Within and express whatever wants to tumble onto the pages. You'll feel healthier too; you'll leave your tension on those pages, away from your mind, and out of your body.

(d) **Why MUST I write this?**

In relating to your intended partner, wouldn't you extend yourself and do whatever it took to be with that person? Similarly, to romance your Writer Within, you must go the extra step and show her how you care. This is when you lean back, close your eyes and ask your Creative Self for guidance. You might hear this:

> *What a shame it would be if this were not written. People will be touched by what you wish to say and your heart really wants to express it. So, do write and allow the highest thoughts to flow onto your pages in love and kindness – so readers will learn to love their Inner Writer.*

After doing all four questions, just watch how your fingers fly over the computer keys, or push your pen over the page. If I'm feeling stuck with my writing, or can't get past the first few lines, this exercise never fails to get me past some resistance and move my writing along.

Try these questions yourself and see how they help to reawaken your passion to write.

Chapter 7. Don't Judge: Accept Her

Would you stay in a relationship with your lover if that person continually judged or criticized you all the time? I sure wouldn't. So, why then would you expect to have a loving relationship with your Writer Within if you judged and criticized the output?

Don't you enjoy being with a lover who laughs at your silly jokes, someone who accepts and appreciates everything about you? In his or her presence you feel better about yourself. Similarly, your Writer Within flourishes with your response, enjoyment and acceptance of her. Your positive response will encourage more creative expression.

In my doctoral research on creativity, I discovered a common denominator in nearly all of the studies for fostering creativity: *let go of judgment* while you are in the creative flow.

Thanks to Dr. Roger Sperry, who won a Nobel Prize in 1981 for his earlier split-brain research,[14] it is now generally known that the two hemispheres of our brain have different functions. The left brain is more dominant in speech, writing, critical analysis, whereas the right brain is dominant in visual and spatial skills. While we need our whole brain to fully function, in creative writing, it is important to engage the right brain *first*, then, edit from the left brain – later on.

Do *not* judge what your Writer Within is expressing because it will stop the flow of ideas; and according to creativity researchers such as Alex Osborn, who developed Brainstorming, the best ideas come last.[15]

Dr. Sidney Parnes, from the Creativity Institute in Buffalo, concurred: "Extended effort in producing ideas ... tends to reward problem-solvers with a greater proportion of good ideas *among the later ones on their lists* [emphasis added]."[16]

Thus, quantity actually produces quality. Why? As you write quickly, more ideas flow onto the page; as you have no time to judge, you by-pass your internal critic. The greatest number of ideas usually leads to the most unusual ones, and uniqueness counts in your stories. Readers want twist in the plots, unexpected happenings and delightful surprises because it enriches their reading experience of your work. So, write fast and see what happens.

To really open this stream of ideas *let go of judgment* during that first draft, so your essays and poems evolve quicker, and your story or novel takes a whole unforeseen turn. Trust it, and write swiftly. Defer any judgment until much later when you're editing and tightening the piece for presentation or publication.

Your Writer Within will enjoy the freedom to express more and you'll probably surprise yourself with what appears on the page. Ask what your Inner Writer would like to express, and then listen, without judgment.

Accept what comes onto the pages. This is what you wrote today, no matter what it is. As your Writer Within "gets it" that you can actually smile at the scribbled words on your white pages, and that you appreciate her wisdom – as well as her foibles – your output will increase.

Play Me Muse

I push your greatness away sometimes
When I feel small and pretend to be big,
Bigger than you;
I ask dumb questions like,
Who cares?
Why bother?
Does this even matter?
What's the point?
But when you hear me and answer,
I always know the truth
Even through my terror,
I feel the soft power in my belly
And my words and music flow out
Until I remember again
Who I really am.

Chapter 8. Call Her By Name

In love relationships don't you often call your partner by a pet name? Speaking the word *Hon, Darling, Sweetheart, Honey-bun, Pumpkin, Lover-boy*, or some other term of endearment can evoke a feeling of love; it's comfortable and comforting, and can make you feel closer.

Why then, would you not name your Writer Within?

She could be whatever you wish to name her. Maybe *Artemis*, Goddess of the Moon, or after some other goddesses. Or: *Suzy or Tamika, or Yoda, or Henry* – just so you can reference her quickly, and you don't have to say "Writer Within." *Jaya* is the name I use, and when I speak that, or ask her advice, I am always answered.

How did I arrive at the name, Jaya? It was after a particularly deep session with a powerful spiritual healer. I'd had such a blissful time and ventured profoundly into the recesses of my psyche, that I felt the presence of a Guide. The healer asked me what the Guide's name was and I said out loud: *Jaya*.

Shortly after that amazing session, I began to write from her, and although that was many years ago, I still have a loving relationship with her, and have written a couple of books with her guidance. She is a combination of my Higher Self, my Creative Self and my Writer Within, and I value her input greatly. She is really why I am writing this book – so I can assist you in mining the gold within your own Creative Self.

Writing with your named Writer Within will help you to reawaken your passion to write – because you will realize that you are not writing alone, and that you can always call upon her. Try it yourself. Just as you named your child, or your cat or dog, your Writer Within needs a name. Then, observe how much closer you feel, and how much easier it is to write.

Simply close your eyes, breathe deeply for a few minutes, then breathe normally, and just sit in silence for awhile. Ask your Writer Within for her name, and it will come. Give it time. Even if it doesn't come immediately, ask the question as you venture into sleep. Trust. The name will come.

To further your relationship with your Writer Within, speak and write loving affirmations on a daily basis. *Affirmations* in this formal sense are repetitions of certain phrases, spoken or written over and over, until they sink into your subconscious mind and re-program all the old, habitual negativity that has resided there.

Here are a few examples of some affirmations:

* My Writer Within (put in your name for her) has awakened and is supporting me daily.

* My creativity is bursting out of me, carrying my projects to new heights.

* My writing is getting better and better every minute.

* My writing flows easily and effortlessly onto the pages.

* My writing is published and highly acclaimed.

* I deserve to be published.

* My Writer Within (Jaya) and I are partners and together we write beautifully.

Make up your own affirmations and write them down. Keep them by your bedside and post them on the walls where you write. Self-statements work. They simmer in your subconscious mind and will gradually, over time, change your mind. Affirmations are a boost to your morale and to your self-belief.

Your Writer Within will love hearing them, too, because as you come to believe the affirmations, you're more aligned with the Inner Truth that she knows.

In midlife, are we not all seeking truth and integrity? Our dedication to our writing can lead us there.

Chapter 9. Understand Her Creative Process

In any relationship, there are ebbs and flows, ecstasy with falling in love, then sometimes, disagreements, frustrations and feeling out of love. In good marriages, notice that partners stay with their process even when it's uncomfortable, because they know that seeing each other through it builds a stable foundation for the relationship that in turn supports their individual growth.

To romance your Writer Within, there are steps or stages, based upon **the four main steps in the creative process.** [17] **These steps are:**

1. Preparation;

2. Incubation;

3. Illumination;

4. Verification.

If you know these steps, you can understand and work with them, instead of feeling hopelessly, inexplicably stuck in your writing.

1. *Preparation*

You decide that you wish to write a piece, say, a novel, a short story, a book of essays, and then you create the environment where you can write. You do whatever it takes to open up to receive ideas, whether that be gathering your pen and notebook and going for a walk in nature; or cleaning up your desk and creating order to make room for your creativity; or keeping a notebook by your bed so that when your Writer Within presents the idea you are able retrieve it. Your mind is opening up to new possibilities.

Consider how a woman expecting a baby would probably create a nursery, look at baby-clothes, take good care of herself because she's about to become a "mom;" would generally prepare to receive that child. Similarly, you must prepare to receive your creative ideas; otherwise, they will escape – vanish into the ethers from whence they came. If you don't have a notebook and pen to receive them, you might not be able to retrieve them again. Preparation is crucial.

2. Incubation

After you begin your project, you have a general idea of what you would like to say, but often, the key component feels elusive and you just can't put your finger on it. Well, the work is germinating, incubating; cooking. Just like when you bake a cake: you put all the ingredients into the bowl, stir, then pour into a pan and put into the oven – then wait the required time while those ingredients transform into a real cake. Ah, what a lovely scent as they're cooking.

But, in this process of creativity, this lovely scent may not feel so good. Yes, you mostly believe that you can write this piece, and you've got the right ingredients – knowledge, intuition, perseverance, desire, intention, writing ability, and great ideas – but will they actually cook and transform into your book or your story?

This can be a frustrating wait. Unfortunately, it is just part of the process. Remember that baby? Well, as you know, it takes nine months to gestate that child. It may not take that long to gestate your project, but it might take longer than you want it to.

Trust that you will get through it. This is when your Writer Within is doing the transformational work. You are not working alone here, you're in partnership, and your intention and commitment will give this project beautiful form – if you allow yourself to partner with your Writer Within. This is a huge part of the creative process.

> *"It is not our task to determine the meaning or substance of a story in advance. Thinking about it is as likely to take us away from its essence as toward it....It is best if we can get out of our own way to find a rhythm that elicits the story in us."*
> Deena Metzger [18]

3. Illumination - or Aha!

Eureka! You've got your answer, the one you've been waiting and hoping for. The moment where you KNOW it will work! Your Writer Within has spoken and you are well on your way now.

Yes, this is a very exciting moment, and very often you will be inclined to sit at your computer for much longer than you ever have before, because you *just know what to do now*, and where your project is going. It all falls into place. You say, "Thank you, Writer Within!"

Still, there may be anxiety that arises at this breakthrough moment. Often, our *Aha* experience can also scare us. Dr. Rollo May addresses this in *The Courage to Create*: "The world, both inwardly and outwardly, takes on an intensity that may be momentarily overwhelming." [19] Now that you have received this awesome idea for a story, or a book you've been struggling with, you feel the sense of responsibility to put it into action. Here's where self-doubts may niggle their way into your mind, or the Critic comes a-calling and you wonder if you are up to the task at hand. *Can I really do this? Can I carry the book through to the finish? Do I have the energy, or the time to actually write this?*

Yes, it can be intimidating and scary. However, that huge realization of Aha can lift you up into such a higher realm that you feel carried by some other "force," or energy. Most likely, this is your Writer Within, and if you tune in and trust her, you can write together – passages you never would've believed would come through your pen!

4. Verification

This is where you need feedback from others. You really want to hear that you are on the right track – or not. (Ooh, you don't want to hear this, but it's a part of the creative process.)Give the piece time, like your newly baked cake, to sit on the counter and cool. Don't even look at it for a day or so. Then, return to it and read it through – lovingly. Pencil in any changes/edits you want to make. Make those changes.

Next, give it to one person you trust totally. This is a gentle human being who is not going to slay you with criticism, but will give you honest – and kind – feedback. Loving objectivity is important, not only for the person giving the feedback, but for you in receiving it. For this reason, you should consider that the person you choose may not be one of your family members. Family relationships carry the added weight of history, need and multiple roles; it's important to remember that our family ways of relating, however supportive they may be, cannot always be mutually objective.

By way of illustration, I learned this myself, the hard way. After I wrote my first novel, I let my brother read the book, and then to celebrate, I hosted a dinner party for 12 people. When I asked him across that table, "Well, what did you think of my book?" He said, "Your dinner is superb." Thinking he hadn't heard me, I asked again and he said, once again, "Your dinner is superb." Suddenly, I couldn't eat. While he was trying to protect me from negative comments, I would have preferred a more supportive response. But hey, brothers don't always give sisters what they want, eh?

Choose a person whose opinion you respect, then, *make an appointment with that person to discuss it.* In other words, make time to receive and understand the feedback, without distractions and without rushing. Just as a parent makes time to talk to her child's teacher, or a couple makes an appointment to discuss one partner's diagnosis with the doctor, so you love and respect your project by making the time for this step.

This part of the verification process is crucial because if you just hand it to someone in the publishing world and are rejected, you may never know why – and that can be dismaying.

Eventually, with step-by-step feedback, your project will be ready to go forth into the world. Then, no matter what comes, rejections or not, you just keep on going. Persevere. Keep sending it out and *seeing* it published.

Chapter 10. Make Time To Meditate

No matter how much you love your partner, you need alone-time to strengthen yourself, as well as the relationship. May Sarton writes about this: "There is no doubt that solitude is a challenge and to maintain balance within it a precarious business. But I must not forget that, for me, being with people or even with one beloved person for any length of time without solitude is even worse. I lose my center. I feel dispersed, scattered, in pieces. I must have time alone..." [20]

Allow your Writer Within that time to just be in the silence. Just BE.

Often, we attempt to control our Inner Writer, or to write when we don't want to. Sit and do nothing. Swallow the silence. Feel it flow down your gullet and slowly slip into the too-tight confines of your belly. Breathe deeply, it is inside you now. Ah, be still and you'll begin to feel at one with the energy Source around you.

I meditate every day because if I don't, my energy gets scattered. Often, as I am slipping into meditation, I'll ask a question about a writing project, and the answer usually comes easily as I open my eyes.

During one meditation I asked Writer Within to write something about Creativity, and this is what came out...

> *There are many aspects to creativity. It is to venture into the mysterious, beyond the mists; to lose one's footing, to find one's divine connection. It is to feel you're being obliterated in order to reclaim the wide-eyed wonder of the child. It is to feel young despite your age. It is to feel, despite your forays into "hell," washed and clean and innocent. It is to be carried, then, lifted up when the circumstances of your life are too dense and heavy. To struggle through prickly foliage of a thick woods and suddenly have the branches part, and you find you are in a sunny clearing with rolling pastures and sparkling light on the green hills beyond.*
>
> *In creating, you become a divine messenger, for when you write words, they have the power to transport you, as well as the reader, to remember that you all have gifts to give; that*

you are a gift. A gift all wrapped up in different shapes, sizes and ages, but a gift to delight and move others.

In reflecting upon creativity, you may finally realize that you do have a lot to offer others; that by doing this, you are contributing to your world - a world that may often appear dark or fearful. By venturing into the silence, by taking Time to ponder, by valuing this sacred space, you trek into the sooty coal and bring forth diamonds; priceless diamonds for they are the shining lights of your souls.

And when you turn those shining lights on, your world may start to glow with a radiant energy that will radiate out what you carry inside your hearts; love...By just allowing your creativity, you are contributing to peace on earth.

Remember, allowing time to meditate is a gift you can give yourself each day. So, take time to be still. Obviously, my Writer Within responded to my query – and yours will too.

Chapter 11. Speak Truth

In a healthy relationship, when you both speak your truth you empower the partnership to grow more solid. When you "own" all aspects of yourself and present them to your partner, he or she will know that you're not hiding anything. Trust grows.

As you encourage truth to flow onto the pages, your Writer Within knows that you want to be aligned with her.

Even if you pen things you don't want to hear, write them anyway. You might write about how you've been playing nice (which we women are encouraged to do) and Writer Within is tired of that. Suddenly, you find yourself writing about the times when you've turned your back on people, or how you were mean to your partner, or how you yelled at your kids, or how you felt jealous when a friend got published before you – or whatever. As you write, you will know yourself better and your writer's voice will be filled with integrity. Writer Within desires truth.

Writing truth, however, may feel like you're stripping your clothes off in public and running around naked like you did when you were a child. I confess I speak from experience...

...When I was a little girl of two, because nature was calling, I had to remove my little sun-suit and pee, right there on the path near our house. Then, I sauntered along – with my clothes over my arm. Mother did not approve: "Come in here young lady!" she yelled. So I was spanked and put to bed for the rest of the afternoon. But, I remember feeling so free.

At 12 years old, I was skinny dipping in a northern lake with my girlfriends, until the owner of the dock we were diving from yelled from his cottage, "Get the hell off our dock!" Oh, how we cracked up on that one. It didn't stop us. We took our boat to an isolated island, sat sunning like little mermaids, and waved at the steamboats sailing by – forgetting that the passengers were probably peering through their binoculars. Oh, we were free. Somehow, being stripped of any constrictions in-between ourselves and nature really was an experience of freedom.

Telling the truth in our writing can free us. While I'm not saying to run around naked, I am stressing the choice for creativity over conformity; to respect your own individual truth; to be willing to dive into your own uniqueness.

In his insightful book, *Creativity and Conformity*, Clark E. Moustakas says, "One cannot grow according to one's own nature unless he is free, and to be free is to accept oneself in totality, to respect one's individuality, to be open and ready to engage in new experience." [21]

We hold back on expressing our truth, though. Why? Perhaps we still fear we'll upset someone, like our mother or father, or at our age, our children or grandchildren. Or, that we're just too naked for all those judging eyes who will read our stuff.

Trying to hold back wears you out. Once you put pen to paper, once you've written what wants out, you're released. You are free! As Dr. Gene Cohen writes in his wonderful book *The Creative Age*: "Creativity is built into our species; innate to every one of us ... It is the flame that heats the human spirit and kindles our desire for inner growth and self-expression." [22] Let go and let the flame of your creativity heat your spirit – so your passion can flow.

Call of the Wild

It's the call of the wild, pulling at your blood
Yelling at you to remember all those times before...

Before you got so structured
When you had no idea what you would do tomorrow
Let alone in the next hour,
And it was okay. You were so alive!

Oh, maybe tears came
And you fell into the lonely holes
But you kept on going.
Some nights, you might listen to music
And dance around a candle for three other people...

You'd laugh and let people in
There was nothing to hide then
No control to maintain
Just like a wild horse, you ran with it.
Hopped on planes,
Flew off to Nassau or Bermuda on a whim.

Whatever happened to that?
Have you laughed out loud lately?
Have you danced wildly, or
Been held in a passionate embrace?

Have you held a man's hand?
Or a child's?
Have you listened to your lonely voice
Calling to you in the middle of the night?
Listen. Oh, please listen!

Chapter 12. Have Courage To Express The Pain

In relationships with your partners, don't you feel closer when they share with you a challenging time in their lives? Their self-disclosure gives you more permission to express your truth to them.

Similarly, if you allow *yourself* to be real, to own your pain and transcend it rather than running away from it, you have much more to offer as a writer.

When the love of my life left, I felt like shriveling up into a ball and stuffing myself into a dark closet for the rest of my life. But I had three teenaged children to look after and had to keep going. So, what I did was this: Every day I would write out the pain I was feeling; it was all I could do really, but putting it down on paper seemed to exorcise it. In several weeks, my pain transformed its ugly head into a book of poetry, entitled *Love Leaves*. The writing of it transformed me. And it was a time of communion with my Writer Within.

Writing does take courage, but it's worth it.

The more you en-*courage* your Self to write whatever wants to splash onto the page, the stronger you become; you face your fear and *move ahead.* As Rollo May said, "Courage consists not of the absence of fear and anxiety but of the capacity to move ahead even though one is afraid." [23] In his earlier book, the influential *The Courage to Create*, Dr. May wrote, "In human beings courage is necessary to make being and becoming possible. An assertion of the self, a commitment, is essential if the self is to have any reality." [24]

Assert yourself and pen your painful experiences to paper. By courageously facing your fears you will release them from your psyche, reawaken your passion, and open up wider avenues to your Creative Self.

Chapter 13. *Write Love Letters*

Letters allow you to read and re-read and really remember the depths of your feelings for your loved ones.

Write to your Writer Within, all the unrequited love you feel for this wonderful writer-self - as if your beloved partner were writing it to you.

Address it to:

Your Name,

The Famous Writer At

Your Street Address.

Mail it.

Upon retrieving the letter from your mailbox, sit down in a quiet place, sip your tea and read it slowly, but eagerly – as if you had never seen it before. It's better than an email. Then, tack it up on your wall. Read it daily. Your Writer Within will love it.

Write a letter back from her:

Close your eyes, be very still for a few minutes, and imagine what your Writer Within looks like. Then, put your pen to the page and let her "speak" to you in a gentle, loving manner. Take several minutes to do this – and you'll begin to realize that you're not alone in your writing process, but that you are deeply loved. For example:

Dear One,

I am so pleased that you have asked me to communicate with you. Let it be a communion, with our highest thoughts meshing to create words that will touch your readers. Let it be a joyful experience, so you know that even if no other person reads what you have written, you will have opened to something deeper and truly fallen more in love with yourself. That in and of itself is worthy of your time, is it not? Then, put your pen to the page and I will be there with you.

Don't you know how much you have to offer in your writing? Can you but open your eyes to all the people you are going to inspire with your words? You deserve to take this time to be reminded of your gifts and talents.

Always know that I am with you and that you can call upon me any time.

Love,

Jaya, Your Writer Within.

Chapter 14. Ask: What Truly Has Meaning?

If you don't spend any time with your romantic partner, it might indicate that you don't value him/her. It might mean that you just haven't looked at your priorities, or that you are out of touch with your own value system. To honor any relationship, it is crucial to examine these thoughts.

Same thing with your Writer Within: You need to write down what really means anything to you. If your writing doesn't even make the list, then stop right now - you're not inclined to hear your own thoughts. But if it is up at the top of your list, then make time to do it, no matter what comes onto the page. Practice improves your writing. Give yourself the time to do just that. You might write something like this...

Does my writing mean anything? If so, why do I constantly put it on the back burner? Why do I make dates with friends, attend so many luncheons or concerts when I haven't given time to my writing today? Will it truly mean anything to me if I write my stories? Will anyone read them? Ah, but if I don't write them, what will that mean? That I am out of integrity with myself? Or will it mean that I don't really trust myself to put interesting words on a page? Have I so lost myself that I no longer trust what I have to say?

Carl Jung, the great psychiatrist, experienced vast turmoil in his midlife, and by reflecting on his own journey he contributed enormous insight: "But we cannot live the afternoon of life according to the program of life's morning – for what was great in the morning will be little at evening, and what in the morning was true will at evening have become a lie." [25]

Kathleen Brehony, in her book, *Awakening at Midlife*, addresses issues such as how we deny ourselves time for reflection; in not taking time to contemplate our lives, we seldom reach an understanding of who we are – who we are destined to be. She says, "The symptoms of midlife are a wake-up call. If they were not so severe, so disruptive, we could easily dismiss them...But our psyches will not have that. The deepest, most authentic part of the soul is crying to be heard..." [26]

If our soul is "crying to be heard," we must listen and address that cry. Both Ms. Brehony and Dr. Jung indicate that midlife can raise our consciousness and that within it, we can experience transformation. Therefore, learning to engage and commune with your Creative Self will assist you in that transformation. As you write you will learn more about whom you truly are, what you desire from your life, and what you wish to contribute to others.

After asking yourself the hard question, what truly has meaning, and writing through some answers, you may find yourself compelled to respond to the experience...

> *I am so grateful that I have made time to sit here and write out whatever I'm thinking. Also, I know I have some terrific stories to tell, and so I'm now more aware of what my writing means. It is a lifeline, a best friend, and the more I spend time doing it, the more I love how it feels. And the closer I get to knowing my Writer Within. I must be changing. I hope so.*

James Hollis, in his book, *Finding Meaning in the Second Half of Life*, speaks of what Carl Jung meant by the term "individuation:" "It is a service not to ego, but to what wishes to live through us... freedom is found, paradoxically, in surrender to that which seeks fuller expression through us. Enlarged being is what we are called to bring into this world..." [27] Communicating with your Writer Within is communing with your *enlarged being*.

May Sarton writes about *meaning* in her journal as she addresses the fact that she is a middle-aged woman with no family, lives in a house by herself, and writes about how she is being responsible to her own soul and how that means something. "The fact that she is a writer and can tell where she is and what it is like on the pilgrimage inward can be of comfort... my responsibility is huge. To use time well and to be all that I can in whatever years are left to me." [28]

> *... in the second half of life meaning is only present when he or she is listening to the Spirit within, the inner voice.*
> *James Hollis* [29]

Write out what has meaning for you. What do you value? What matters? Then, trust your words, for they will lead you by the hand to reawaken your passion.

Chapter 15. Say "Yes" More Than "No"

Imagine if you kept on saying "NO" to your partner: "No, I don't believe you. No, I don't want to see that movie with you. No, I don't like your ideas. No, not tonight..." Well, what do you think would happen? The energy of communication would get sucked out of the relationship. It would contract rather than expand.

Say "YES" to your partner, say "YES" to your Writer Within, then notice what happens.

Even if you're overloaded at the moment, at least jot your idea down, give it a file name on your computer and then come back to it later. Or, create a three-ring notebook for it; quickly write out the piece, then put it in that notebook. But do not ignore it.

"YES" moves energy forward.

If you have an idea for a story or a book and something in you shrieks, "No, you're already over your head, so don't even think about it," you can imagine what happens with that brilliant flash. If you persist in thinking this way, you may start to feel exhausted, and feel even more upset that your children have left you in an "empty-nest." "Oh, what's the point, it will never go anywhere!"

When you ALLOW the idea and those feelings to come, it's a different story: Say "YES;" give them a voice and you honor your Inner Writer. "YES" brings more creative output. "NO" shuts you down. "YES" says you love and value your Writer Within.

YES will awaken your passion.

"If you have passion, there is no need for excuses, because your enthusiasm will trump any reasoning you might come up with."
Dr. Wayne W. Dyer [30]

Chapter 16. Reject Rejection

Would you give up on love because you've been rejected a few times? Well, perhaps you would, that's a choice you make. But with your Writer Within, you must never give up - otherwise, your dreams will die.

As Langston Hughes, the great American poet, reminded us:

> *Hold fast to dreams*
> *For if dreams die*
> *Life is a broken-winged bird*
> *That cannot fly.* [31]

Let your Writer Within know that you will treat her with respect, honor her gifts, and will never reject her. This will provide a stronger sense of confidence that you are working together, and will continue to do so. Remember, the only way you can fail is to quit – and you're not going to do that.

Read how others have been rejected, so you are inspired by their stories to keep on going. Jack Canfield and Mark Victor Hansen had 144 rejections on their first book, *Chicken Soup for The Soul*. Imagine!

They persisted, obviously, and we all know what happened: they shifted their own attitudes, and a little-known publisher took them on. So far, they have sold 115 million books in 41 languages. Seven of their books were on the New York Times Best Seller's List, at one time.

In a recent interview with Steve Harrison, a book-marketing genius, Jack Canfield said, "We make our own luck... You've got to believe that what you have is very valuable, and if you don't give it, you'll be depriving others of this gift... You have to decide to succeed – and cut off alternative paths. Expect success." [32]

Often, after several rejections, some writers expect to fail, so they don't bother sending their work out. So, hold onto Jack Canfield's words: "We make our own luck. We attract good things into our lives." [33]

The highly successful writer, Barbara Sher, experienced "failure" for several years: at 44 she published *Wishcraft* – but it took five years before it was issued in paperback, and then gradually, slowly, took off; 30 years later it is still selling well. That did not make her rich. Ten years later, at 54, she published *Teamworks!* And she was 59 when her third book was published, *I Could Do Anything if I Only Knew What It Was*. Her fourth book, *Live The Life You Love* won a first-ever self-improvement book award. Her fifth book, *It's only too late If You Don't Start Now*, is where the following quote originated, in a section entitled *Failure*...

"The book you're now reading is due to come out when I'm sixty-two. I hope it does well, but I'm through with predictions. That's what failure has taught me." She adds that she just keeps "plugging along" because she likes to write.[34] Twelve years later, Ms. Sher is still writing, enjoying it – and inspiring me, as well as many other women, I'm sure.

Her positive attitude motivates thousands of her readers, as well as all the people who participate in workshops based upon her books. She writes: "As far as I was concerned, I had lost the battle for success and developed a lot of respect for the unpredictability of fortune. After that, I did my part and forgot about the rest. That's a very relaxing way to live" She affirms that this gives her "an unending supply of daily energy." [35]

Take the attitude of Barbara Sher, Jack Canfield, and Mark Victor Hansen to heart: it will assist you, whatever age you are, to reawaken your passion to write, and eventually to publish.

Chapter 17. Appreciate Her

When you appreciate and acknowledge your lover, that person feels expanded in your presence because he/she knows they are loved. They feel as if you are on their side, as if you are growing your relationship together.

So, appreciate your Writer Within and see the beauty of what she offers.

In Webster's Dictionary, *appreciate* is defined thus: "to recognize gratefully; to estimate the quality or worth of; to be fully or sensitively aware of..." [36]

Recognize and be grateful for your own writing. Read it over and see it lovingly. I did this the other day – read one of my own novels and was blown away, or should I say that my self-doubts were! Suddenly, I saw this writer, me, with new eyes. That new perspective restored my zest.

Even if your submissions for publication have been rejected a lot, keep on going. Your stories, poems, novels, non-fiction books and essays deserve to be read. Take time, not only to read them over, but to acknowledge them. If you do not love and appreciate your own work, how can those creative babies live? Nurture them so they can venture out with strong legs.

Be on the side of your Writer Within. Re-evaluate the quality of your writings, and if necessary, edit and tighten them up. Sometimes, if you have had too many rejections (I've sure had my share!) you will then need to reassess how you can be published.

One way is to invest in self-publishing. It will give you a sense of completion, and a finished product to hold in your hands – a book to market anywhere you go. Be the boss, the Master of your own destiny. Be pro-active and bid the poor little rejected "victim" farewell as you take your writing out to the world. Recognize and be grateful for what you have written, and all that you will continue to write.

The on-line market is huge now, and thousands of new books are published that way. Try MyLulu.com or iUniverse.com. Try marketing one of your books as an e-book. Or, you can photocopy one of your own books, create a nice cover for it – maybe one of your own photos or paintings – then, have it spiral-bound. It's inexpensive and you have a book to market.

Books that were originally self-published:

I Googled this topic; delighted to discover a four-page document by that name. Here are a few of those books: [37]

* *The Celestine Prophecy* was self-published by James Redfield. Rejected by mainstream publishing houses, he chose to publish himself, and sold copies from the trunk of his Honda – 100,000. Then, Warner Books decided to publish it, and bought it for $800,000. It became a #1 bestseller in 1996, and as of this date, 5.5 million copies have been sold.

* *The Elements of Style* by William Strunk, Jr. and his student E.B. White. Originally self-published for the classes he taught at Cornell in 1918, it sells more than 300,000 every year and more than 10 million have been sold.

* *The Self-Publishing Manual* by Dan Poynter, who has been named "the godfather to thousands of books." Since 1979, 190,000 copies in print and 15 revised editions.

* *When I Am an old Woman I Shall Wear Purple*, written by Sandra Haldeman Martz, was published by her own publishing company, Paper Mache Press, 42 times, and has 1.5 million in print!

As Dr. Gene Cohen says in *The Creative Age*, "The secret of living with one's entire being... is the creative spirit that dwells in each of us. It is the creativity that empowers us, no matter what... The unique combination of creativity and life's experience creates a dynamic dimension for inner growth with aging." [38] So, appreciate and be grateful for all your years of experience, for they have given you more riches from which to write.

May Sarton, in *The House by the Sea*, reminds us: "The great thing with any creative work is that it is never repetitive. The problems are always fresh, one is never bored..." [39] So, you can take your time, see your book project lovingly and trust that it will emerge into fruition – and you can self-publish it!

In appreciation, your Writer Within will sweeten your heart and smile inwardly.

Chapter 18. Lovingly Reward Her

Would you stay in a relationship with someone who never said one kind thing to you? Or work for a boss who mistreated you? Perhaps you would in your twenties, but not now. I hope not. Hey, be kind to your writer who works for you.

Give her rewards:

* For writing one piece.

* For researching where it could go.

* For the query, and then, for sending it out.

* For finishing that story you started last week.

* For writing another chapter in your book.

* For writing in your journal that day.

* For writing that overdue letter to your friend.

* For sitting at your desk despite your urge to procrastinate.

Ponder ways in which you could gift your Inner Writer - then, do it. For example:

* Take a nice walk in the park near your home.

* Go for a swim.

* Sink into a hot bubble bath.

* Sip a latte at your favorite coffee house.

* See a movie with your best buddy, etc.

Stress will fall away and you'll be able to hear the loving voice of your Writer Within, and she will work with you!

Go a step further with your appreciation:

Buy her some lovely things to remind her how serious you are about working with her. Besides, don't you love to give presents that symbolize your love – to your children, your partner, or your friends? Give gifts to your Writer Within:

* You might purchase a beautiful three-ring binder to hold the book you are writing,

* Or an elegant pen,

* A little knick-knack for your writing area,

* A new lamp for your desk,

* A ring that reminds you that you are a writer,

* Or maybe a new computer...

Every time you look at these objects, you will smile as they remind you that you are a writer, a successful one, too. So what if you're not yet published, you're on your way!

Loving your Writer Within will expand your relationship and your writing will flow onto the pages much more easily as you work together. Your passion will flow through your blood stream and fill you with great exuberance.

"This is why I say that the presence of passion is so critical. It doesn't just help us emulate the all-creating Divine mind; it allows us to become one with it again."
Dr. Wayne Dyer [40]

Chapter 19. Feel Your Feelings

In any fulfilling relationship with a partner, it's important to feel safe enough to express what unspoken feelings are really going on between you. Expressing those feelings will dissipate any stuck grievances or upsets; you will clear the waters and sail through those challenging situations with love.

Your Writer Within wants you to express deep feelings.

Your Journal is a safe place to do that, and you get to really feel things as you pen them into your notebook. Through my journal every morning, I can write my way through most feelings of anger, sadness, disappointment, frustration, annoyance, or fear, as if I am speaking to a therapist. Usually, I resolve the negativity and start the day off on a better note. Writing in a journal every day can provide real comfort.

Taking the time to write in your journal is a sacred sharing time with Self; a date with your soul; time spent with a best friend; it is a soul-dive. It is the place where you can write anything you wish, where you can resolve issues you don't discuss with anyone, where you can emote and "let it all hang out." Your journal is always there with you, ready to receive whatever junk you wish to scrawl into it.

In *The Seat Of The Soul*, Gary Zukav asserts that "When we close the door to our feelings, we close the door to the vital currents that energize and activate our thoughts and actions....Only an awareness of your feelings can open your heart." [41]

Let the tears flow. Let the anger out too – and notice how hard you are pressing onto that pristine white page; don't worry, it can take it –and you will feel so much better afterwards (after words). Write out those deep feelings. Put them into another character in your story if you choose to, but let the feelings surface.

In soul-diving deep into your journal, you practice writing your feelings, and your Writer Within will reveal more and more to your open heart. Within that closeness, you will be empowered to write pieces you never dreamed you could write, and you'll be in awe of what comes forth.

Here in the 21st century, when people are saturated with digitized information, they crave to be moved with emotion, with empathy. It is a timeless human desire in any century, for us all to join together, sharing experiences of the heart and spirit, rather than mere intellectual bonbons. Great writing moves us within. Great writers go to the places where they are raw, where they dive deep into the oceans of their psyches and experience and come up with pearls; unique pearls of pain, suffering, fear, understanding and healing; through these, we all grow in understanding.

Brewi and Brennan affirm, "The task of journal writing can create the ferment necessary for new insight and creativity. It can break open the bindings around our heart and allow us to cry out for the structure we need to be free... Keeping a journal allows us to find the new patterns for acting out our true Selves." [42]

Practice expressing your deep feelings into your journal – so you won't be afraid to write them into your stories and novels. Not only will your eventual readers benefit from these authentic expressions, your own passion will be reawakened.

One needs to get in touch once again with one's past enthusiasms and the images of oneself that once drew all of life's energy toward them and set one on a new road in life.
Brewi & Brennan [43]

Chapter 20. *See Her Wide-Eyed Child*

Gaze at a photo of yourself as a child. Yes, you're in midlife, or beyond that, and you may have raised your own children, so what good is this gazing going to do? When you look at the child you used to be, you reconnect with your own sense of wide-eyed wonder and innocence. While you can often see innocence in your partner, it's more challenging to see it in yourself.

When I looked at one photo of myself at five years old, I cringed and felt my heart constrict: there she was, that child of a dysfunctional family, and in her eyes was pain. Finally, I wrote a song to (and from) her, and here are four lines from that lyric:

I look in the mirror for the girl I used to be
And see instead an older face gazing back at me
Where did she go, the one so young so free?
Child of mine, come back to me."

Writing that song greatly helped me to reunite with that disowned aspect of myself – and I can now keep that photo right here on my desk. That little girl speaks to me and through her I feel even more love for the child I was then. My heart opens up. I don't have to block out the sadness anymore.

With all that energy now freed up, my writing improved, too, and I gained much insight. Even more, as I dialogued with her...

Dialogue with your inner child:

When you dialogue with your partner or friend, you can resolve issues and feel closer to each other. Similarly, when you dialogue on paper with your inner child, you can reclaim a huge part of your self; for even when you've consciously disowned an aspect of yourself, you still carry it, like a heavy suitcase filled with childhood memories. But when you do the work of embracing it, you get to unpack those memories, toss out the old suitcase and free up your energy.

This is what a dialogue might look like on paper...

Me: I'd like to get to know you so we could work and play together.

Child: I don't know about that. You've ignored me for years.

Me: Please, can we talk?

Child: What about?

Me: Look, I'm sorry if I hurt you by ignoring you, but I'd like to make it up to you. (I close my eyes and see a little girl hiding out in a cave. She is not happy.)

Child: You abandoned me when...

This goes on for two or three – or seven – pages, until your inner child gets out her annoyance, and you can feel her coming closer to you... Until finally, she truly believes that you do love her. Sometimes, your inner child might be feeling very shut out, so don't expect it to be an easy conversation. Take the necessary time.

Turn on some soothing music and put a photo of that child upon your desk. Just gaze at it and continue to write. This will help you heal with this persona of yourself, and at the same time your writing will improve. If the tears come, or deep sadness, don't hold back from feeling those feelings; they will heal you, and you will have more of yourself to write with.

Venture into yourself and clear those pathways to your creativity. You will reawaken your passion to write.

Chapter 21. Rewrite History

You bring all of your own history to a relationship with your lover. Often, those past events, experiences and decisions can prevent good communication, and block the flow of love - unless you become aware of your early history and set out to resolve its hold on you. Hey, by midlife, there is a lot of history! Just as we saw in the exercise with the little child within you, negativity or shame about more mature experiences can also drain your creative and loving energy.

Early in your life your Inner Writer might have been shut down creatively. Based upon some adult's thoughtless comment, the innocent, creative child you were made a decision that your work just wasn't up to par. That decision probably blocked the flow of your creativity for years!

But you can restore your wounded Writer Within! Something that can work well is to rewrite your creative history. For example...

Perhaps you were told by a teacher, when you were nine years old, that you couldn't even do finger painting, or you were shamed when your picture wasn't "good enough" to be pinned up on the classroom wall. You can rewrite this creative history.

Suggestions for rewriting your history:

1. Begin by writing the true story of how your painting was not put up on the bulletin board, and how sad or upset you felt at that time, and how angry you were at your teacher, Miss Smith. Or how you felt dismissed, demeaned or deeply hurt about your creativity by some adult.

2. Then, let your imagination run wild and have its way with you as you fictionalize the middle and the end of your story – and rewrite your history. Here is where you have fun! You might write about how a great artist comes and visits the class, and your painting is voted The Best and awarded a silver medal.

3. Allow your imagination to really take over: Another fictionalized scenario might be that your favorite Auntie Lily mounted an art show of all of your paintings and everyone in your community came, and were "wowed" by your art. (Doesn't that just make your energy soar?)

This is rewriting your history. When my students have done this exercise, many have had amazing shifts in their perceptions of their own creativity. They were then able to release huge blocks and venture deeper into a new story or book.

Deep within your psyche Writer Within will smile – and welcome the creative play. It will give great joy to your inner artist and you will notice changes in your own writing.

Try this exercise yourself and you'll be delighted at what emerges onto the pages. Go on, write up the worst creative experience you ever had, and then play with it, fictionalize it, rewrite it into something empowering. As you change that past experience, it will change you.

> *... creativity demands your soul. Search your soul to determine if you are using full capacities as a creative individual, or if you are over-relying on others.*
> *Annette Moser-Wellman* [44]

Chapter 22. Examine Your Resistance

In any good relationship, it is important to examine anything that might be blocking the honest flow of love, so your relationship can grow and support each of you in it.

Your Writer Within will also benefit by examining any resistance you have to expressing your creativity fully.

In her wonderful book, *Women Who Run With The Wolves*, Dr. Clarissa Pinkola Estes wrote, "To bring back creative life, the waters have to be made clean and clear again. We have to wade into the sludge, purify contaminates, reopen the apertures, and protect the flow from future harm." [45]

I heard Dr. Estes speak in Vancouver several years ago. She said her book was a labor of love and shouldn't be read in a hurry – because it took her twenty years to write it. So, you need not be in such a hurry to write the perfect book. Hers was a best seller for months, but she gave it the necessary writing time that it deserved. You can learn from her, as I have done.

I highly recommend her book. I have constantly used it in my workshops since it was first published in 1992, because it is timeless. Read Chapter 10, "Clear Water: Nourishing the Creative Life."

Here are four questions that will help you to examine and release any resistance to your creativity:

For the first three, dive as deeply as you can into the negative aspects. For question four, be positive:

1. What I think of creative people...

2. I would let myself be really creative, if only...

3. If I let myself be really creative it would mean that...

4. I am willing to see the truth of my creativity; the truth is...

When you write your own answers to these four important questions, you will get a clearer picture of what might be holding you back in your creative output. Write at least a whole page of responses, and write them very quickly - so your critic doesn't have time to hold you back.

I encourage you to do the exercise yourself, before reading the rest of the chapter. There are some very common answers that come up over and over among writers, but give yourself the chance to hear your own. And then we'll discuss how to use this crucial information.

Here is what some of my students have written over the past twenty years in response to these questions:

1. What I think of creative people is that...

* They are uncouth.
* They don't live in the real world.
* They are irresponsible children.
* They have no time to clean house.
* They're flighty and air-headed.
* They can't pay their bills.
* They're selfish and arrogant.
* They think that the world revolves around them.
* They're a little weird.
* They dye their hair strange colors and dress strangely.
* Airy-fairy.
* Many never make it in the world.
* Too far gone to care.
* Too esoteric.

We always have a good laugh as we share our lists, and then we discuss what these knee-jerk ideas really mean. If as a writer you think that these are traits of a creative person, then how successful will you be when you attempt to write? How can you be a creative person if you believe that this is really how a creative being is?

However, in identifying these caricatures lurking in your subconscious mind, you can counteract them with many more positive, attractive thoughts: that creative people are exciting, clever, disciplined (they have to be if they're going to get their books out there), and they can, if they persist, earn income from their writing.

Responses to #2: I would let myself be really creative, if only...

* If only I had more time
* If only I had more energy
* If I wouldn't feel so exposed when my work goes out there.
* If only I wouldn't hurt my family by what I say.
* If I could only avoid the secrets.
* If only I wouldn't hurt my kids.
* If only I didn't have to work at my boring job.
* If only I weren't so old.

* If only I had a partner to support me.

* If only I have more money in the bank.

* If I could believe that my books were really going to sell.

* If only I didn't feel so stupid about writing certain things.

* If only I had more to say.

* If only I didn't have to support my family.

* If only I trusted the process more.

* If only I had more discipline.

* If only I were really creative.

* If only it wouldn't upset anybody.

Responses to # 3: If I let myself be really creative it would mean...

* I'd expose too much of myself and feel naked.

* My work would probably hurt my mother.

* I'd hurt my husband.

* I'd embarrass my children.

* I'd have to hobnob with famous people

* I'd end up doing drugs.

* I'd have to top my own creativity, and that would be tough.

* I'd be criticized mercilessly.

* I'd have to become a celebrity, so how would I find the time to write?

* I'd have to keep on being so creative.

* I might burn out.

* I'd be too busy.

* There'd be no time for a relationship.

* I would probably have to move - to hide out.

* I'd probably say something I don't want to say.

* I'd be harassed.

* Embarrassed.

* I'd be shamed.

* I'd be ostracized.

* Nobody would love me.

* I'd have to live alone on a desert island and hide from the world.

* I'd be too rich and I wouldn't know who was truly a friend - or whether they were just after my money.

For those first three questions, it is important to "wade into the sludge" (as Dr. Pinkola Estes suggested) and clear it away – so the stream of creativity is made fresh again. Those old negative thoughts actually dictate how your writing goes: whether you allow yourself to be successful or not; whether you actually sit at your desk and write another book – or whether you feel like quitting. When you identify these old thoughts, you can bring them to the surface, look at them honestly, and take control of them. At least they are now conscious and you can deal with them realistically.

You can go over each one of those old thoughts, and turn it into a positive possibility.

For example:

"I'd expose too much of myself and feel naked." This could now become, "I am willing to expose of myself only what I feel comfortable with, and let my writing come forth. Besides, I could always write under a pseudonym."

"Nobody would love me." could evolve into, "I have dear friends who love me no matter what— so this is not true."

"I'd have to keep on being so creative." This could turn into, "Now that I have been so creative, I know how it feels and it feels great— so I know I can keep being creative."

"I'd have to hobnob with famous people." When examined carefully, it might mean, "Hey, this isn't so bad. I might like hobnobbing with a few famous people."

"If only it wouldn't upset anybody." This could become, "My creativity won't upset people if they really care about me."

Responses to #4: I am willing to see the truth of my creativity, and the truth is... (be positive in writing answers to this question).

* It's my salvation.

* It keeps me going.

* It's my best friend.

* It's my connection with the Divine.

* I love myself in my creativity and find a greater Self there.

* My creativity gives me joy and excitement.

* I experience awe from it.

* I absolutely love it that I'm creative.

* It feeds my soul.

* It takes me deeper into myself.

* I am willing to go through anything and everything to express it.

* I trust it.

* I welcome it.

* I am grateful for it.

Now you can see that when you write out your own answers to this question, you will really know what the truth of your creativity is. Now you will be inclined to write more because you will know why it is so important to your life.

This is a clear way to honor your Writer Within and expand your relationship with her.

Every time students have done this exercise, I have done it too – and although that means that I've probably given responses hundreds of times, I have always benefitted from it – and let go of some last bits of self-sabotage that were choking my writing.

Have fun with the exercise and as you release your own creative blocks, watch your creativity speak up freely. Remember...

*"Feared, creativity atrophies. Distrusted, it shrivels.
Refused, it slinks away."*
Deena Metzger [46]

Chapter 23. Release Self-Sabotage

Have you ever sabotaged your love-relationships? Often, that nagging critical voice will say: "This isn't working," or "I want out," or "He doesn't see how great I am," or "She is dragging me down." But if you pause and acknowledge what that voice is trying to do, you may be able to sustain your relationship.

That voice is the Critic, the ego-self. It will attempt to lead you away from union with your great Self. Why? Because if you surrendered to your Creative Self, your ego-self believes that it would have no voice at all.

What self-sabotage means in creative work:

It means turning away from the very gift you are given. It is spilling yourself down into such a negative puddle that you slosh out there on the sidewalk, rather than entering the sacred space of communion with the divine energy that will lead you forward. It is when your Critic attempts to sabotage your Writer Within.

How does Critic do this?

* Dismissal of your work.

* Criticism that your work is not good enough.

* Perfectionism - it will never be what you wanted it to be.

* Manifesting reflections "out there" of your own inner fear – such as an agent's rejections.

* Dragging your feet, so you don't take your writing project to the next level.

These are points where the greatest battles occur: within yourself, puffed-up ego-self against your Creative Self. Even though you have progressed to actually writing quite well, this self-saboteur may try to stop you from taking the next necessary step.

Your Writer Within wants you to win, and if you allow that, she will lead you to success.

So, what to do?

* Write a letter to the Critic. Let it know that you have appreciated its help but that you are letting it go now.

* Sit still, meditate and ask for the truth. The truth is that your work is good and it deserves to go out to the world.

* Steward your project; see that it is delivered into the right hands, an agent, or publisher, or a loving editor who will help move it forward.

* Create a Master Mind group: Here, you are held accountable, and your friends in this group give you "tough love" to get the work out there.

* Meet with one trusted friend and give this person permission to "call me on my resistance." In the Introduction to most books, you will notice it takes a team to get the book out there.

* Recognize that there are many voices within you, but you must be the Director of your play, and call forth the voices that best support you.

* Write a letter to your Writer Within and give her permission to be in charge. Let her win.

* Open your heart and create the space, silence and willingness to work together. Do not scoff at this, but be willing to engage in the process of co-creating. When you engage, it opens wider the doors of possibilities, where you choose to create with more energy.

* Align with your Creative Spirit and allow her to work with you. Trust that she will - if you ask and really want that partnership.

* Ask your Writer Within for support and she will happily give that. Remember that you are not working alone in your creative endeavors.

Remember what Jesus is reported to have said in the Gnostic Gospel of Thomas:

"If you bring forth what is within you, what you bring forth will save you.

If you do not bring forth what is within you, what is within will destroy you."

Chapter 24. Make Peace With Other Pieces

When you share some of your past experiences with your lover, you deepen your communication. Sometimes, you might get out the photo album and point out some funny times you've had in your life. You can laugh together.

Your Writer Within will also love this exercise. So, gather up your photos and look carefully at them...

Oh, who was that teenager with the funny hairdo? Was that hippie actually you? What an experience you had that wild weekend – at least, judging by the expression on your face. Look at that trip through England with that crazy Italian, Marco. Who was that person on her wedding day? Were you really a mother so young? You look like a kid yourself. How were you feeling? Who were you then? What would that person in those photos want to say to you?

Write from those personas – and you'll begin to remember just how many stories you have to tell. You'll also dive a lot deeper into your own psyche, retrieve long-forgotten memories and bring to consciousness a huge dimension of your life.

As women, we have denied ourselves to look after others, our parents or our children, our partner, or our good friends; and so we've tucked the pieces of our lives back into dark closets - and sometimes forgotten the strong, powerful, dynamic aspects of ourselves. Write from these personas, and you will reclaim those wonderful facets of your life and start seeing your full self with more love and appreciation.

When I have framed funny photos of myself in different stages of my life, and written from them, I have owned those strange-seeming personas and added more to my writing arsenal.

As you examine your own photographs and write from them, your Writer Within will embrace the experience, and probably nudge you to do more. You might even discover novels in those photos, and your story characters will also have more quirks and qualities to enliven them.

Writing in this way is fun, surprising, and will lead you by the hand back to your home of passion.

Chapter 25. Love That Former Self

As you embrace any former persona and the one you are now, you are more able to love your partner – because you won't be expecting him/her to fix you, or love you into being happy. If you expect anyone to fix you, the relationship is doomed from the start. But if you do your inner work and learn to know yourself, you have that much more to offer to a partner.

And as you love the writer of you, you are more capable, more open to loving your Writer Within.

Here is a personal example of this learning:

Way back in 1998, I had spent several months writing a book about dialogues with my higher Self. I was trying to market a proposal for it – which was rejected – and I was ready to tear out my hair. That rejection made the pile of other rejections just too high – including a novel I'd spent eight years writing. I took an emotional nosedive and dallied in despair. Perhaps you know the feeling?

A dear friend of mine, Deb, kindly listened to me and then reminded me to love myself. That was very hard to do in that moment, as all the fears of aging, hot flashes and insomnia of mid-life were crowding my psyche as well. So, how did I get through that time? By writing my way through it – and in the end I was able to rise up and view myself with brand new eyes.

Here is some of what I wrote:

She was a vulnerable soul who fell to the ground like an acorn from an Oak tree and allowed herself to be split and rendered open – in order to begin the process of new growth, as a new tree, pushing roots down into the black soil; staying in that dark for awhile and then rooting herself and growing up out of the underground.

She took the journey into the underworld and came up with pearls of wisdom. She trusted her inner Self as her guide and sank into the darkness every day to let go and let God win. And she did thrive in that darkness. She just sat and meditated for long stretches of time. And out of that, she wrote some good pieces from her Creative Self. She allowed her personality to shrink in favor of her soul. She trusted that she would be all right – and in the end, she was/is.

I received many gifts from "her." She was a soldier in service to her soul; a warrior doing battle with the demons that threatened her extinction. She was a pilgrim venturing through lands of terror, and untrammeled mountain ranges that tore at her feet. I saw her set sail like Columbus, towards new lands, exploring wildness, meeting greater obstacles than she could ever have imagined – and grappling with them until she was victorious. Yes, this woman won. This woman kept me (the little me) alive. This woman is my benefactor and I owe her a huge debt of gratitude. This woman held up the white flag of truce and surrendered to truth – and lived to tell the tale.

So, this woman is to be loved and cherished. This woman experienced the pain of birthing, of pushing and ripping open and bearing down – until she saw the face of her Self. And in that face was all the love she had been seeking in others, all the love of a trustworthy parent who was there for herself. And now as I write about her, I can love and welcome her, let her know just how great she truly is – for she has the face of God.

Try writing about yourself as if you are "the character" in your own book. I know how my own experience healed me then, and I continue to use this type of writing often. It puts me back in loving relationship with my Writer Within. When I wrote that journal piece, I "got it" and my passion for writing was restored.

Chapter 26. Forgive

Forgive yourself: When you carry anger and resentment towards yourself – which midlife women, or older women do, because you have been taught to be nice and hold back your true feelings – you run the risk of projecting that onto your partner, and it can erode the love in the relationship.

Similarly, when you carry that lack of self-forgiveness into your writing, you have a much harder time communicating with your Writer Within; a barrier is built so that your little ego-critical-self is on one side and your Creative Self on the other. Thus, it is important to examine your internal dialogue about this, return to those pertinent situations when you chose to make yourself wrong and bad; when you decided against yourself. To be in alignment with your Writer Within, it is crucial to forgive.

So, here are a few scenarios from a writer's life that might sound familiar:

Remember how you didn't follow up with that agent you met at the conference several months ago? Yes, now, he's probably forgotten all about you, so your chances of working with him are about zilch. And that time when you got distracted by the lunch date with a good looking man, then hurriedly mailed that essay to the editor ...only to later find six mistakes in your draft! Or, when you just couldn't seem to finish that project you'd worked on for so long, you finally gave up on it? Or when you decided you had to have a fancy dinner party on the chance that this famous producer passing through town would accept your invitation? Yeah, right in the middle of writing a film script, putting on the Ritz wrecked your writing – and the invited Famous Producer didn't even show up! On and on it has gone; all those darned mistakes you've made with your career.

When I first moved to Los Angeles, a new friend hooked me up with a top agent, who said, "I'm sure I can sell your script as a TV movie of the week." But I puffed up like a peacock and made the mistake of my career: "Oh, I wrote it as a feature, not a movie of the week." After too many additional drafts, that "feature film" still sits in my filing cabinet. For ages, I beat myself up with my stupidity.

We all have our own litanies of missteps and bad judgments, and sometimes they can cost us in self-esteem, especially if we simply cannot forgive ourselves. In my own life, I turned to some spiritual reading, and discovered a wonderful series of books called *A Course in Miracles*. They led me to make a decision: To let it go – and forgive myself.

> *Forgiveness is the key to happiness. Here is the answer to your search for peace. Here is the key to meaning in a world that seems to make no sense... Here are all questions answered; here the end of all uncertainty ensured at last. (CIM, Workbook)* [47]

After a long meditation, I pondered forgiveness and asked my Writer Within to speak:

My dear one,

Now, through forgiveness, you are on the other side: You can choose to look back in fuller comprehension and with greater love and empathy for yourself – and then, turn your eyes forward – for you have much to do, gifts to give, love to embrace others, as well as yourself. Allow the Grace of this understanding to fill you up, so you realize what a great spirit you are, and how much you have to give.

For too long now, you have been denying the truth of who you are. Love yourself – your Self, and know that you have a great life yet to live, people to touch, to remind who they are. You are a bright light and your spirit wants to shine forth into the darkness. Please, let it shine.

I recognized then that I was doing my best to "shine my light." I felt so much more peaceful after that process.

Forgiveness is not a one-shot deal, but an ongoing request from your heart, to open yourself up to seeing how innocent you truly are. It is about loving yourself – your Self – and remembering what a beautiful life path is still in front of you. All you have to do is take one step at a time. When you do that, your pen will lead you to wonder and awe, and your passion will reawaken.

Forgive others too:

You can heal your relationships with loved ones this way. Forgive those who have rejected or emotionally harmed you in your personal life. If you are carrying grudges against some former lover, your resentment will be picked up by a potentially new relationship and might well affect it negatively. It is crucial to forgive others, as well as yourself.

Remember The Law of Attraction in the movie *The Secret*? Basically, it means that you will attract to yourself whatever vibrations you are emitting from your own consciousness.

In your writing life, if you are carrying old anger towards some agent, or editor or publisher who didn't seem to appreciate the writing you were offering, that energy will continue to fill you, and attract even more rejection.

In L.A. some colleagues and I had the opportunity to meet with an agent in his sixties, named Ben. When I spoke excitedly of my wonderful musical film script, Ben's bushy eyebrows rose up high and he guffawed loudly: "*Musicals! Musicals! Who's ever heard of a musical coming out these days?*"

My face burned with shame as everyone laughed. But the following year, two musicals debuted to accolades: *Cabaret* and *New York New York*. (So what did ol' Ben know?) I'm sad to admit that I carried resentment towards that man for several years – but it certainly didn't help with marketing any of my future work. So, I once again turned to A Course in Miracles:

Anger is never justified... Pardon is always justified. It has a sure foundation.... Forgiveness is the only sane response. (Text) [48]

Forgiveness offers everything you want. Today all things you want are given you... Retain your gifts in clear awareness as you see the changeless in the heart of change; the light of truth behind appearances. Be tempted not to let your gifts slip by and drift into forgetfulness, but hold them firmly in your mind by your attempts to think of them...(Workbook) [49]

So, I made a point of forgiving Ben – and myself, for carrying that resentment for too long – and my heart opened wider to even better ideas. Then, my Writer Within softened my soul, which helped me through the writing of several books.

Once again, I wrote from Writer Within, and this is what emerged:

Dear One,

Can you not but remember that I am here within you and I am guiding you forward, no matter what your life looks like. I am your vision, your highest thoughts, your light in the darkness, and as you shed even a little beam onto the path ahead, it will illuminate your steps and lead you forward. Trust this. Yes, even if you cannot see what is ahead, please do not forget the work you are doing, for it is important. And remember how much I love you and how much I want you to succeed in all your efforts.

Love,

Jaya (Writer Within).

Chapter 27. Dream Big And Clarify Your Goals

In a good relationship, you and your partner can grow together by discussing and clarifying your life's vision.

Regarding your writing, Barbara Sher writes: "Midlife is the first time you have the luxury – or the desire – to go after the dreams of the unusual, one-of-a-kind person you really are." [50] So, it's about thinking big and opening up your heart to what you really want in your life.

In an earlier chapter in *It's Only Too Late If You Don't Start Now*, Ms. Sher discusses Freedom: "Real freedom means the right to be who you really are. It's the freedom to go for your dreams, and to rediscover your original self that got buried under the seductions of achievement and family." [51] She says that the greatest freedom, the one that counts, is to live our lives with our heart, mind and emotions open wide. To keep on learning

– and to "treasure your childlike sense of wonder." She stresses that it is this freedom, and only this kind, that makes us young again. [52] And who doesn't want that experience? To be revitalized, your passion reawakened. To *open* your eyes and heart and soul to your *childlike wonder*.

Through this openness, when the dream is clearer, you can work in smaller segments and create smaller goals. Write what you'd like to accomplish by a certain time. When you write them down they happen – this is the power of intention. Once you are clear about what you desire and you put it "out there," that definite intention sweeps a path in the universe and establishes a focused course of action.

Dr. Wayne W. Dyer, in his book *The Power of Intention*, says: "An apple blossom in the springtime appears to be a pretty little flower, yet it has intent build into it and will manifest in the summer as an apple. Intention doesn't err." [53]

Your Writer Within will resonate with your dreams and your intentions. As you state your project-goals, that Inner Power will impel your writing forward, keep you on track, and work with you to manifest these goals.

Goals are dreams with specific dates upon them:

"I will finish my book by... this date."
"I will send my book to the New York agent by... this date."

Sometimes, it can feel nerve-wracking to have these goals specified so definitively because it may sometimes feel like pressure upon your creative mind. But a dead-line is actually a life-line, and you'll begin to feel like you are progressing towards your dreams – when you live up to these goals.

Remember, you are not working alone, but with your Writer Within.

"Goals and prospects for the future flow from and emerge from the new sense of true identity." [54]

Chapter 28. Share Your Stories

As you share stories with your lover, your relationship strengthens with the self-disclosure and you can deepen your love this way.

In the same way, as you open up to receive old stories tucked away in the recesses of your mind, your connection with your Writer Within will deepen.

In a passionate book, *Urgent Message from Mother: Gather the Women, Save the World*, renowned writer and activist Dr. Jean Shinoda Bolen asserts, "The stories that stay with us are another form of soul nourishment... Nourishing the soul is essential to staying on your course, as is finding meaning in what you do." [55]

The following exercise will help you to write your stories: and you will access the right hemisphere of your brain (while temporarily by-passing the left!) ...

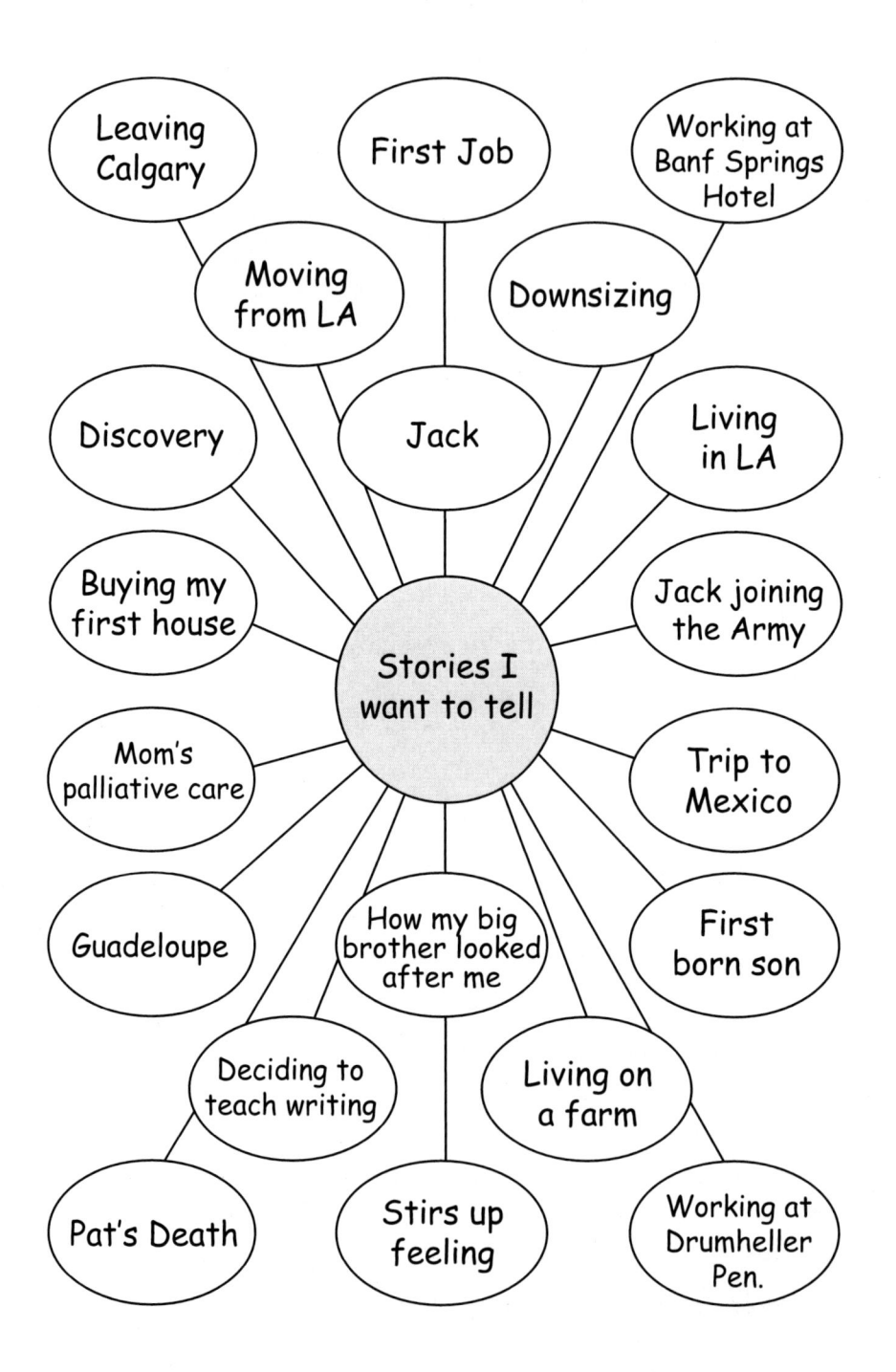

Share Your Stories

Stories I want to tell

- Leaving Calgary
- First Job
- Working at Banf Springs Hotel
- Moving from LA
- Downsizing
- Discovery
- Jack
- Living in LA
- Buying my first house
- Jack joining the Army
- Mom's palliative care
- Trip to Mexico
- Guadeloupe
- How my big brother looked after me
- First born son
- Deciding to teach writing
- Living on a farm
- Pat's Death
- Stirs up feeling
- Working at Drumheller Pen.

Draw a circle in the middle of a page and inside it, write the words, "Stories I want to write." Then, draw little lines out from the circle and add smaller circles – somewhat like little balloons. Then within each balloon-circle drop in one idea for a story, and then, another and another as you fill up your page. Gabriele Lusser Rico, in *Writing The Natural Way*, terms this "clustering." She says, "A cluster is like an expanding universe, and each word is a potential galaxy: each galaxy in turn may throw out its own universe." [56]

As you look at this page of messy circles, some of the words in those circles will stimulate your imagination and remind you of specific details regarding those stories. Or, they will lead you to places in memory you thought totally buried. Sometimes you can use all the circles to write from, and other times, you reach a memory that brings you to an "aha" moment and that is what you choose to write.

The other evening, in a group with my students, I was writing about "time" but after clustering, I wrote about polishing my brother's soldier boots – and then, how he died before his time. It totally surprised me to go there. I'll share it with you, unedited ...

I polished his soldier boots when I was 13

*I laughed when he came home that day with a Mohawk hair cut
And a black India ink 8-ball tattooed on his bare skull.
At the dinner table, I watched and listened to the knives and forks clattering on our plates; and the terrible silence as we waited for Father Vesuvius to erupt.
Then it happened.
"What do you mean you joined the army? When?"
"Today."
"How?"
"I walked into the enlistment office, right there on Main Street, next to the pool hall, signed my John Henry."
"You're only 17."
"That's why I need your signature."
"You're too young."
"What am I going to do here? Wait around till you clout me again? till I cut down another wrong tree?"
I remembered the 60 year old Maple he'd hacked down a month ago; the one beside the diseased one.
Mom's English lips tightened, strung taut across her red face.
Dad paused, looked over at his first born son, then stuffed more red roast beef and mashed potato into his mouth.
The clock ticked loudly...
Finally, Jack said, "Well?"
A loud sigh from Father, then, "I'll sign."
So my brother left school, no more playing hooky, no more rockets into the school parade.
He fought in Korea.
Time away - too long...
Time away too fast
As I gazed at his body in the coffin, aged 56
Where did his lifetime go?
Why do I still write about him?*

Choose one story a day, or per week, and write it up. Remember, your stories are important to tell. As you and your Writer Within conjure up more of these, your excitement will grow and you'll recognize the gifts you have to give.

Over the past twenty years, hundreds of students have worked with this exercise and have been amazed at how it stimulates their right brains, and how deeply they tap into old memories to write incredible stories – that totally surprise them with what they express.

I encourage you to try this and see what comes out onto the page. Cluster for about five minutes and then write for ten. I promise that you will be astonished at what you write. And your Writer Within will love it.

Chapter 29. Treasure Map

Your imagination is able to form clear pictures of what you desire, so visualization is an important tool. Some people use this technique to create relationships; they cut out pictures of an attractive man/woman and see themselves with someone who reminds them of that pinup. Others may use it to create new homes, or you may do this to see your newly published books on Chapters' bookshelves, or to visualize your title on the marquee of your favorite theatre in the city.

In creating a treasure map, images are imprinted upon your mind that can eventually lead you to where you really want to go.

A friend of mine, Scott, now a retired M.D., cut out a photo of a beautiful home by the water and carried it in his wallet for months. Well, upon moving to a small city near a huge lake, he dug out that photo – and was stunned to realize that he was living in that exact home.

So, get yourself a large piece of Bristol board, several old magazines, scissors and a glue-stick. Sit at your table and cut out the pictures that you are intuitively drawn to, whether or not those images make logical sense to you. Remember, the only criterion for choosing an image is that you just like it, that it inspires you or makes you feel happy. (Your Writer Within will be smiling!)

Then, glue them onto the cardboard in a collage – with cut-out words: "You can do it," or "Yes, this is my dream," or "I am being interviewed on *Larry King Live*," or "It's wonderful being on the *Oprah* show."

Put this treasure map up in your home where you can see it every day – you might wish to tack it up on the back of your closet door, where nobody else could poke fun at it. These pictures will inspire you to move towards the images. This is your map towards your treasure. Instinctively, it will bring you closer in touch with your Writer Within, and your imagination will be working day and night as you ponder it. It very well might lead you to a partner in life, too.

In *Secrets of Becoming a Late Bloomer*, authors Goldman and Mahler tell us that many research studies show that any creative pursuits will probably improve our physical health too. And that we can actually redesign our lives through the use of our creativity. In doing so, we are given "easier access to our imagination, intuition, and inner dreams... When we engage our imagination, a sense of the possible beckons us forward... the human spirit is revived, restored, and filled once more with hope." [57]

When we have hope our passion can find its way back to us.

Chapter 30. Continue To Hear Her Stories

In sensitive and loving relationships, your partner takes time to listen to your stories, even though you might have told those stories a few times over. You create space to hear your partner, too – because as human beings we have a need to tell our stories, sometimes again and again; not so the other person will hear us, but so we will hear another facet, another aspect to our own story. As each person listens to the other, safety is re-established, healing happens; closeness grows.

You also need to tap into a depth within yourself that allows you to access your Writer Within, so you can heal another facet of yourself. A couple of pages back, I wrote (again) about my brother, Jack, who died too young. Although I have told that story of polishing his boots many times, and have remembered myself doing that at age 13, when I put it into this book, I felt yet again the twinge in my chest of missing my big brother. In that moment he is real and present to me, and I want the world to know him.

Sharing the stories I have of his short life honors his memory; ensures that he has never been forgotten, no matter how many years he has been gone. But it does more. In writing about him this time, something awakened in me: an idea to write a book about him, or a series of stories? Perhaps that sudden heaviness in my heart is calling me to follow my pen on the page and see where it takes me. I know that in the writing process, we understand more deeply – so following this call might allow me to "become" him and let him speak, as a character in a story or book, through me.

Through trusting my Writer Within, I was guided here to allow my story to simply appear on these pages; I followed my heavy heart and wrote. I trusted that this is where I needed to go today. It was not planned, it just happened. Spontaneity is a way of an artist, but it is also a way of living that will open you to more awareness, and will awaken your passion to write. If I had put a cap on my creative expression just now, I would have shut some deep feelings down, and blocked this story from this book. But I want to engage all aspects of myself, and offer more to you, the reader. Life is a lot more intriguing then, isn't it? (Besides, my Writer Within made me do it!)

Tristine Rainer speaks to how when we recover our lives through writing our autobiographies and memoirs in her highly informative book, *Your Life as Story: Discovering the "New Autobiography" and Writing Memoir as Literature*. Ms. Rainer asks that age-old question: *What is a story anyway?* Then she elaborates about how as children we "gobble them up and never feel too full for more," and she discusses that myths and fairy tales are stories, as are movies, novels, and sit-coms; but that we cannot quite get our hands around what story truly means.

She emphasizes this: "The individual stories of our own lives tell us who we are and infuse our personal existence with excitement, meaning, and mystery... However, the stories of our own lives require active searching, learning to look through our memories in a new way." [58]

Search your own memories for your stories, bring them to the surface and feel them, taste them, smell them, savor them – and write them. You will be richer for the experience of doing so – and your midlife challenges will morph into channels from past times that enliven and expand your whole life.

Chapter 31. Truly See Her

In a relationship, when you really see your partner, not just looking, but really seeing who he or she is, you open up the lines of communication between you.

In writing, if you can open up to seeing what is before you, extend love to that object or person, then you can project yourself and feel as if you've become that object.

In doing this next exercise, you will learn to write more interesting characters in your stories. And your Writer Within will delight in the love involved in this exercise.

Upon reading a wonderful book by Frederick Franck, *The Zen of Seeing*, I was inspired to bring some of his insights to my writing groups. Although his book is about drawing, it still relates to the artist within, and expands specifically the ability to see – an important skill in any creative expression. Franck says, "I have learned that what I have not drawn I have never really seen, and that when I start drawing an ordinary thing I realize how extraordinary it is, sheer miracle...All that is, is worthy of being seen, of being drawn." [59]

Substituting the word "drawn" for the word "written," this exercise opened students up to truly being in the present moment.

> *"I have learned that what I have not written I have never really seen, and that when I start writing an ordinary thing I realize how extraordinary it is...All that is, is worthy of being seen, of being written."*

Based upon Frederick Franck's ideas on drawing, I suggest you do this exercise:

(a) **FIND AN OBJECT** that you might want to write about – any object in your own home.

(b) **CONCENTRATE ON IT** for a few minutes and pretend you have never seen this object before in your life. LOVE that object, project your feelings so that you absolutely fall in love with it.

(c) **CLOSE YOUR EYES** for three minutes and remember it.

(d) **PUT PEN ON THE PAGE** and focus your open eyes on the "love-object." Gaze at it as you would your lover.

(e) DESCRIBE this object as if you are drawing it. Try not to look away from it. If it is a plant, simply write about one leaf, one tiny aspect. Write as if you've never seen it before in your life, with the excitement of discovery; make it brand new.

(f) BECOME the object and write as if you are the thing. You ARE this lamp, or this cat. Write as if it is speaking. (Become your lover and see how much closer you become to that person.)

(g) DIALOGUE with the object: The lamp may be talking to the piano or your shoe - or you. Go back and forth as if the two things are having a conversation. It's fun and easy – and your writing will really come alive this way.

Here are some examples:

(e) Describe: This is about a tiny bird on a blue vase.

Tucked in there, white body, pink head, there is a wild look in your eye,
Your mouth is open and I see your body crisscrossed with lines –
Feathers fluffing up against the royal blue, you grip the brown perch
With huge finger-talons, as if you want to fly, but aren't yet
ready to do so. Ah, why fly, you say, it's so cozy here, so safe;
perhaps tomorrow.
Besides, the glazed curves surrounding you are part of the design
And if you left, everything would change. So why leave? Besides,
the beauty you bring to this inner world offers this eye a feast so
delicious it begs you to stay.

(f) Become the Object: Write as if you are the thing.

Continuing with the bird on the vase...
Ah, so you think it's easy poised here, ready to take off
When everyone around will be damned mad if I go...
No wonder I'm upset; yes, you would be too.
There's so much here to stay for.
But my heart yearns to get out of this place; just to see where I head.
I've heard the Dahlias tell of their seed-flight from California,
And Rose says Seattle is far enough. But I hear tell of my darling mate twittering away early in the morning here; reminding me I could go far.
Oh, to look down on this house from a way up in the sky
Makes my heart just yearn for Home.
Okay, tomorrow, I'm going.
So don't be surprised at the hole I leave, eh?
Until then... see you. Look up and I'll be there.

(g) Dialogue with the Object:

Hey Coffee Pot, you're in my way. How can I get out of here if you block my way?
Oh, China bird, who do you think you're kidding. You're not going anywhere.
What makes you so sure?
You've been in the same place for years.
Well, we all change you know!
Not you my friend. You're permanently ensconced.
Not so... It just looks that way.
How on earth are you going to leave your pals, when you're all squished into the same world?
I told them I was leaving.

There'll be a hole then.
How come? You don't know.
I sure as heck do!
What makes you so sure?
If you leave, everybody's world will change. There'll be a gouge in the dam, the water will run out over everything, the roses will die and the table will be ruined – the whole world will fall apart. Oh, get out of here coffee pot. You're just jealous. All you do is hold coffee!
Okay then, go for it. At least I'll be intact, and Missy won't lose everything. But if you ask me, you're a darned ungrateful bird.
Oh, get off it, you old pot.
Okay already. But I'll be here when you crash and there's nowhere else to go.
You think she'll be really mad?
Wouldn't you if your world fell apart? Think about it.
Okay, okay, if you put it that way... maybe I'll stay.
Okay, I'll stay.

Thus, from one small bird on a vase and one coffee pot, a story can evolve. Your Writer Within will enjoy this imaginative exercise and you will truly begin to see in a new way. Also, all kinds of characterizations will fill your pages and delightfully surprise you.

Try the exercises yourself. Look around your home and find an object that intrigues you – then, write about it, and become it. No matter how old you may believe yourself to be, this will catapult you right back to being a kid again – and your creativity will blossom.

Chapter 32: Remember, She Is Your Friend

My daughter said of her husband: "He is my best friend." Relationships have a much better chance if the partners are friends; within that friendship, love can grow much stronger. It's the same thing with your Writer Within; being friends is crucial.

A pal of mine who was having some challenges with his new home – floods, near-fires – said that the only thing he could do was to write about those negative experiences, and he realized in that moment that "writing is my best friend."

I feel the same way: For years I have felt very close to my writing and have often asked questions of my Writer Within. One day I again asked Jaya: What about Creativity? And this is what I received...

Creativity is that which flows through you at every moment – and yet you need to also be quiet to let its presence be known. Every child is born creative. But during the school years, teachers pay most attention to drumming ideas into heads, rather than drawing them out. True education comes from the Latin root of the word "educare" which means to draw out, or draw forth.

One needs to be quiet and allow whatever wants to emerge to come forth. There are also other methods that will stimulate one's creativity... Sometimes that means opening up to new perceptions. Looking at something from a different point of view; seeing the same old thing differently. In this way, the creative mind can then make something so mundane and ordinary –extraordinary.

If you study your hand, you will see that there are tiny hairs on it, marks you never noticed, or veins on your fingers you weren't aware of. Simply going to a new place will assist you in seeing differently – and in this way, you can write or draw a hand that is different than anything else – something unique and original.

Creativity is a vast topic: For now, take what you have and think about it. Study your hand, then sit and write about it in a way you never have.

I asked: But why do some people not open to their creativity?

Expressing one's creativity can be a truly exciting time in a person's life. It is a time for reflection and contemplation - and certainly, a time to be quiet during an allotted time of your day. Have you noticed that those who are so busy only become more and more tense - and they really don't accomplish what they could if they sat and meditated first? Their cups are already filled.

Just as the Buddha taught his pupil in that old story: The master poured him a cup of tea - and then kept on pouring and pouring and the cup overflowed and ran down onto the man's legs, until he leapt up, shouting: "What does this have to do with anything?"

"Everything," the wise Master said: "Until you have emptied your cup, you shall not be able to receive anything from the universal energy; your cup will be too full to receive."

So, empty out. Prepare to receive what is rightfully yours. But your cup must be empty to let it in. If you heed that advice, you and your Writer Within will be close friends.

Chapter 33. *Play And Have Fun*

Don't you love having fun with your partner? Just goofing off and enjoying time together, without thinking or discussing anything significant, will open up your creativity and expand your communication.

It's the same thing with your Writer Within. Play will open up the brain and expand communication with your Creative Self.

Have you watched people playing with their pooches, tossing balls for catch, running with their pets, laughing as Fido leaps up on two legs against them, nearly pushing them over? Sure, you observe others playing, but do you actually do it? Do you play with your creativity?

The other night in a writing group, *we played* with brainstorming – and laughed our heads off as the ideas got crazier and zanier. The topic was simply: <u>List uses for old bricks</u>. And in ten minutes, our small group came up with over 100 ideas – and the last ones were the best.

In Chapter 7, we briefly discussed the power of brainstorming for the creative process, because it encourages imagination, and helps bypass "logical" limitations. It does so via a few simple but absolute rules.

The rules for brainstorming are:

No criticism allowed; piggyback on other ideas; seek new combinations of ideas; and the wilder and crazier the better. Most important: *Do not judge.* [60]

Often, when groups are *trying to* "storm the brain" in brainstorming, [61] someone will say, "Oh, we tried that before," or, "No, that will never work." But if one person just writes down the ideas without commenting, that list will grow. As will your individual creativity.

One of the leaders in the field of creativity is Dr. Sydney Parnes, now Professor Emeritus of Creative Studies at Buffalo State College; fifty years ago he was co-founder with Alex Osborn of the Creative Education Institute in Buffalo. Parnes incorporated the brainstorming method into the Creative Problem Solving program, and his work has acted as a cornerstone for Creative Problem Institutes that are held monthly in various American cities. Prior to Parnes' work, any university studies of creativity were thought a bit weird – a vast difference from today, when you can find Dr. Parnes on YouTube, speaking about how humor is a big part of the creative process: "Humor is "ha ha, and in the creative process, you get "ahas." [62]

Another way to add humor, play and come up with even more ideas in your brainstorming groups is to Maximize, Minimize, or Rearrange.[63] This means to change the ideas you've come up with. For example, if you want new ideas for the uses of bricks, you could maximize and come up with giant concrete blocks. To minimize, you might see tiny brick earrings. To rearrange might mean that the molecules in those bricks could be transformed into another material, such as plastic, or ice cream.

Some of those uses for old bricks were: Castles for fairies (minimizing); box cars bumping in the night (maximizing); space ships for fairies (minimizing); fillings for giants (rearranging); earrings (minimizing); red hot coals (minimizing); iron shavings in volcanic atmosphere (rearranging); red sand between the toes (minimizing and rearranging); atoms flying apart (rearranging); astro-turf for a brick sh- - house (rearranging). You get the picture?

Doing pre and post tests, we wrote stories before and after the brainstorming:

Before, the stories were quite tame: Basic recounting of true experiences in their lives. Not that these were not valuable, but the imagination was not engaged as much.

Afterwards, the stories were wild and exciting: These involved suddenly travelling to Mars, exploring realms never known before, more use of the crazy-wild visuals.

My research has shown that, while brainstorming in a *group*, the *individual* creative thinking abilities of fluency (quantity of ideas), flexibility (different sub-sets of ideas) and originality (uniqueness) *measurably* increased.[64]

Students in that writing group reported that they could feel "something" in their heads expanding – the exercise seemed to physically open up their creative abilities. It was exciting! In this way, we all played, wrote and allowed our Writer Within to express more.

Try brainstorming in a group. Then, observe how your individual creativity expands. Brainstorming will open up the gate to your Creative Self – she will love the joy of it. Remember the rules: No criticism, piggyback on ideas, new combinations are sought, and the wilder and crazier the better. And have fun doing it! Playing like this will reawaken your passion.

Chapter 34: Make Time For Her

In the relationship with our partner, or with someone we really care about, it is crucial to make time for that person. Otherwise, our partner will feel (perhaps, rightfully so) that we don't really care much. People partnered with workaholics may suffer from a sense of alienation and separation, because while the person is there, sitting at the computer in the next room, he/she may not really be present for that relationship.

Similarly, you may be struggling with your own computer, attempting to write your book, put words onto the blank screen, but you are not taking the required time to be with your Writer Within; you may be pushing rather than allowing the flow to happen. This blocks your relationship with your Creative Self. While perseverance is important with your projects, it is not always an invitation to your Inner

Writer. You may be indicating: *"I can do this alone, I don't need your help, leave me alone, won't you?"*

I was in that mode not long ago, so I reached for a book of poems I'd written on Time. Those poems helped me to remember what this very book is about – and my soul was soothed. Yes, you need time to bring your gifts forth.

Jan Phillips, in her inspiring book *Marry Your Muse*, says: "In the process of creating, time is one of the essential ingredients... Time is what we bring as an offering, a sign of our commitment... Making time for creative work is like making time for prayer." [65]

Writing takes time; writing a book takes hours and hours. But in spending that time, while you may be solitary, it is not lonely, for your Creative Self is with you.

Here are two poems I wrote many years ago.

Time is a gift
Time is holy,
Why not treat it so, and live more fully?
Twenty-four beautiful hours a day,
I want to use this gift well,
Not just let time pass me by.

Take the Necessary Time
You most need to love yourself
Without self-love how can you put love into a world starving for love?
It is a choice you make; even in the dark of the night when you cannot sleep; even in your dreams that may startle you awake. Love is the only way a person can open up to the depths and creative ideas within.

You are a creative being, but the circuits of your creativity are jammed
Too much thinking and doing. You must be.
Be.
It is all right to sit and allow your soul to return to you.
Too much of you is spread around on outer aspects, pulling from too Many directions, taking you further away from that light within.
Your soul is calling out to you: "Come back to me.
Please let me be the great light that I am.
Do not cut me up into tiny little candles here, there and everywhere – no. Be one great ball of energy."

Take time to meditate; return to what is truly important.
You can always fix this little corner of your life, or that one,
Call a friend, do another errand, or talk yourself away.
But to remain in the stillness is to honor your soul.

You have many talents to offer this world.
Do not let them ooze out, down your face and into calls about taxes. Balance your worldly needs with those within.
Do you ever give yourself a full day off?

*Stop. Be quiet. Go within – this is what you truly need.
Please listen.*

*Meditate today. Be gentle and quiet,
You will have a stronger sense of who you are, and in this quiet
Strengthen yourself.
The world wants what you have to offer.
Take the necessary time to bring it to them.
But first, bring it to yourself.*

Observe how you spend – or waste – your own hours, then write a poem about time. Awareness reawakens life.

Chapter 35: Commit

A relationship with your lover wouldn't work too well if your values were entirely different – say, the other valued material possessions but you valued more simplicity. It's best to get clear on what is important. Sometimes, it is this clarity that will resolve issues; sometimes, it leads to a healing – or, unfortunately, a severing – of that relationship.

If you are in integrity with your Writer Within and actually live and write according to your inner values, you will have a better chance of sustaining a good relationship. Your work will have a much better chance of being read by others too.

Commit to your Writer Within and let her know you're ready to settle down. State what you really want from your writing, and if it is actually a career. (Sure, you can begin a new career later in life – who says you can't?) Write this out as a contract and sign it. Tack it up and read it daily.

The great German thinker, Johann W. von Goethe, has inspired many people to move forward with his thoughts on commitment:

> *"Whatever you can do, or dream you can, begin it. Boldness has genius, power and magic in it."* [66]

The famous Scottish explorer, W.H. Murray reflected on Goethe's call to action when he was imprisoned in a Nazi concentration camp during World War II. Murray was so committed to writing his first book (on mountaineering) that while surviving inhumane conditions, he wrote it on the only paper there was, toilet paper. When the Gestapo confiscated that book, he wrote it a second time! This man certainly lived by his own declaration:

> *"Until one is committed, there is hesitancy, the chance to draw back, always ineffectiveness. Concerning all acts of initiative (and creation), there is one elementary truth the ignorance of which kills countless ideas and splendid plans: that the moment one definitely commits oneself, then providence moves too. A whole stream of events issues from the decision, raising in one's favor all manner of unforeseen incidents, meetings and material assistance, which no man could have dreamt would have come his way."* [67]

As a writer, you may be likewise inspired to make your own declaration of commitment, such as:

I, Mary Jane Smith, hereby declare that I am willing to let my writing go into the world – my books, my short stories and my poetry. As I make this declaration, I ask for guidance from Source and realize that as I do, I am never alone in my work, but carried by a Greater Force, one that truly knows how to bring my visions and dreams to fruition. I know my intentions are lovingly guided, and that I am always supported in my writing, through sickness and health... And so it is.

Commitment means that when the going gets tough, you don't stop. It means staying with it, persevering; disciplining your self to get to the computer or notebook at least an hour per day – or more. The intention you put into the project will carry you through the down-times; it wants to be written – even if you cannot imagine how it's going to get done.

A botanist friend of mine reminded me that the flowers and plants simply grow in miniscule amounts, and we cannot rush them; they have their own time to bloom. It is the same with our creativity. So, if you do just one thing towards your project, one page, one idea on paper, one chapter, you will eventually complete it.

Besides, your Writer Within may have other plans for your project, and sometimes you need to pause before rushing full-steam ahead. For example, this very book you are reading began as a much smaller book, and seemed to lack heart. And so it sat in my filing cabinet for some time. I needed to pause, re-read it, clarify what I wanted to say – and more importantly, listen for what my Writer Within needed to say.

At first, I was annoyed with the delay because I was about to begin yet another book. But Writer Within seemed to gently shake me and whisper: *"You can do better here, you can give more. Don't you want this to be a book that even you can refer to for your own writing?"*

So, I doubled the size of the book, wove other colors into its tapestry, changed the title, added more specific examples, gave it more thought, and remembered something important…

Just as I want to romance my Writer Within, my Writer Within is romancing me, too.

To commit means to be on the side of your Writer Within. Listen carefully. Ask what she wants you to do. Then, take the necessary time to allow new passages to come. Although it is sometimes frustrating, you will find that overall it is an exciting process. Once you are committed, you will be led by your Writer Within – and that will rev up your passion.

Keep in mind that your passion must be fed in order to survive; it will never let you down if you nurture it. How could it? It is God within you.
                        Dr. Wayne Dyer [68]

Chapter 36. Be Gentle With Her

Although there may be a commitment to your (new) partner, you may suddenly have such high expectations that they're difficult to maintain. You must be gentle with this relationship and with yourself, and allow this love to go at its own pace.

With your Writer Within too, do not impose such heavy tasks, like hours and hours at your desk pushing to complete your book; ignoring friends and some other sweet aspects of your life. Be gentle with her. Your Writer Within is always there with you, but you must allot the time to slow down, take walks, be out in the sunshine; and very importantly, to meditate so you can hear her voice.

Give Writer Within time to BE: just be gentle, and your relationship will work a whole lot better. As I said earlier, give her time to speak to you. She will probably remind you that you are working together, that you're not alone in this process, and that in partnership, your writing will have more heart and be more powerful. Trust this process, then witness how much easier it is.

Here's a poem I wrote that speaks to the topic of gentleness, from a small book of poetry, *Play Me Muse*:

Would you not hold your thirsty soul forth to drink?
Would you not wrap it in a blanket for warmth?
Hold it lovingly to your breast where it can hear your heart beat?
Feel mother-love and know it is safe?
Give it the love it needs?

Then find that in nature.
Be where you can venture out in a boat
Sit calmly: listen to the sounds of the loons as they soar over your head
Be in a green verdant environment that "yeses" you,
Where you can tune in to every tiny daisy and count its petals;
An earth space that grows you.

Time now to create love.
If you love yourself, you will find a reflection of that.
If you give yourself a grand space in which to write,
You will speak truths - and attract them to you.
Remember, you are worthy to create whatever comes through you
Let that be, and love your self in the process.

Chapter 37. Take Her Into Your Bed

Your bed is a place of intimacy for you and your beloved partner.

It is also a sweet space for you and your Writer Within. Before going to sleep, ask her for guidance on your writing for the next day. Keep a notebook next to your bed and expect an answer to some question you have regarding your writing. You will receive it. Your Writer Within will awaken, and write.

One night, I had feelings of "Divine discontent" and I asked, "So what is my Divine Self trying to tell me? Please answer me ..." And this is what came in the middle of the night:

> *My child, do you not already realize how you are pushing the river and not stopping long enough to feel the cool water and see the rushing flow*

of it? Give yourself time to appreciate what is around you. It is all there for you. The sun will shine tomorrow and the breezes will blow softly, so just open to your life. Know that you are guided to all the people and all the situations which will assist you in what you are doing. Trust this.

BE with the feelings and they will lead you Home to more of yourself. Be with this nighttime, and if you feel lonely or isolated or unready for what you are experiencing, just know that those feelings are nudging you forward to your next step. First, feel them.

I slept deeply after this answer, and in the morning, I slowed down, was gentler with this writer, and trusted that all would be fine. And so it was.

When you experiment with your creative power, you prove to yourself that you can accomplish things.
Annette Moser-Wellman [69]

Chapter 38. Be Nice To Her In The Morning

With your partner, don't you love to wake up tenderly together in the morning? So, romance your Writer Within and put pen to paper as soon as your eyes open.

One morning, I awoke with these thoughts:

You are the keeper of a rare present from God; one that indeed has been given to you in trust and in faith - just as a parent is sometimes asked to hold funds in trust for her child. Imagine if that parent actually spent that trust-money? Wouldn't that be a great betrayal, to deprive that child of a gift that would have been hers upon entering adulthood?

Well, in not using the creativity given to you by squandering it, you not only deprive that future generation of the gift, but indeed yourself. If you are not valuing it, if you prefer to store it in a closet with the unused boxes of ornaments for the Christmas tree to be used once a year, that is not enough.

This gift you received was one where the memories of many generations are stored in its cellular memory. You can draw upon that, you can use the greatness of Einstein, or the perception of great artists like Van Gogh, or Picasso. You can use the mind of any great writer, tune into that same place and know that the Great Vault is for your use as well.

But the vault starts to seal when it is not drawn from. It is more difficult to get into it if you forget the combination. So, you must draw from it daily, and realize how it is there for you: a legacy from God. Not to use it is to deprive yourself of something you could utilize for good in the world. Not to use it is a sacrilege.

Please use what is given you. Use it with joy and delight - and let it sustain you! Tune into its awaiting facets and bring joy to yourself and everyone who witnesses that creativity. Do you not think that when you write that it empowers others to do the same thing? Then do so. Let your light shine in this world and you will bring the light of love to the planet. Let Me flow through you and all will be a better place.

Love, Jaya

While you most probably will pay attention to those notes from your Writer Within, you may wonder if the scribbles in your journal are worth keeping. They are: If you journal all of your feelings, your challenges and dreams throughout your whole life, you can go back every six months or so, and read the pages over. You will discover some of your best ideas, poems and stories in there. Highlight them in yellow. Then, type them up in a clean form.

Novelist and diarist Anais Nin, for example, wrote several of her books by rediscovering journal pages she had already written, then compiling them.

I've done it, too. One Christmas time, feeling depressed and overwhelmed by the relentless December rain in Vancouver, I went through my old journals and "found" sixty poems about creativity. Delighted, I filled my days with that project, which became the book, *Play Me Muse*. Written to and from my Writer Within, she loved it! And I reawakened my passion once again to write.

Chapter 39. Give Her Permission To Be Naughty

In a relationship with your lover, knocking down all the negative barriers and getting them out of the way will create more closeness. Being a little bit naughty may also help.

What would you write if nothing were holding you back? Would you type out erotic stuff? Would one of your characters be really bad; a thief or a murderer? What are some of the things you've always wanted to say to somebody who offended you? What is the absolute worst thought you can think of? Write this stuff! It's a huge break-through.

Many years ago, the first time I penned the word *fuck* in my journal, no kidding, my face flamed and my heart pounded – but I was released! I could then write whatever

I wanted to – and my Writer Within was pleased with my hard-earned freedom.

We "nice" women hold our arms tight to our bodies, walk without too much of a wiggle (well, some of us do), and conform to the ways we were taught by our mothers. There's nothing wrong with those conservative manners in society... but in creativity, you must break such attachments to conformity, allow yourself to play and create something new.

In an anthology of essays on midlife women entitled, *Our Turn, Our Time,* Joan Lemieux writes about how we cannot turn to our mothers and grandmothers for advice on the journeys we women are now making, for their challenges, albeit difficult, were not the same as those we deal with. "We are the first generation of women to be given such a long period of time as a 'second adulthood'... more freedom ... greater choices and more decisions. It's a whole new voyage... All sails are up." [70]

In giving yourself freedom to express whatever splashes onto the pages, you also free your Writer Within. And encourage your readers to bust out of the molds they were brought up in, as well. After all, don't you want to reawaken your passion to write? Let yourself be a little naughty and notice what happens.

Susan Martz edited a book of essays on life in our later years, appropriately named after the poem which has inspired millions, *When I am an Old Woman I Shall Wear Purple*:

When I am an old woman I shall wear purple
With a red hat which doesn't go, and doesn't suit me.
And I shall spend my pension on brandy and summer gloves and
satin sandals, and say we've no money for butter.
   "Warning" by British poet, Jenny Joseph, 1961 [71]

Wear purple with red, eat your dessert first, sing in your shower – loudly, if you feel like it, eat with your good china, wear that beautiful nightgown you bought that's still in the fancy tissue paper, let yourself be sexy, buy that lovely dress with a bit-too-low cleavage, get sassy, smile at strangers on your daily walk, tell a few jokes that might be slightly off-color. Laugh more, and BE the woman you were meant to be.

Remember, the little acorn has the potential of a great oak tree in it. And that caterpillar is going to become a butterfly. You too can transform your life. You are the only one who gives yourself permission to be all that you were meant to be, even if it means being a little bit naughty. So do that! Reawaken your passion.

Chapter 40. Encourage Her Sensuality

In a relationship with your lover, it helps to lighten up and play. Or, in midlife, have you forgotten how to do that?

You can romance your Writer Within this way, too.

To stimulate her sensuality, you can:

(a) **Tickle her fancy.**

(b) **Touch with "new" hands.**

(c) **Taste in new ways.**

(d) **Stimulate your sense of smell.**

(a) Tickle Her Fancy with a few silly exercises that will open up your right brain and help you to play...

* Lie under your coffee or kitchen table - and write from there.

* Crawl around your home like a little child. Touch things, lick chair legs, and feel your feelings. I know this sounds weird, but it opens channels to your Writer Within. Doing things out of the ordinary will help your writing.

* Drive home by a different route.

* Use colored pens and doodle in a notebook with your non-dominant hand.

* Eat your dessert first.

Now write, and notice how easily your writing flows.

(b) Touch With "New" Hands:

Whenever you touch your lover's skin, you get to experience a different sensation each time – with palms, finger tips, and even your wrists.

Similarly, when you become aware of the sensations of touch in your daily life – by touching in different ways – you awaken your senses and free up more of yourself so you can open at a deeper level to your Writer Within. Use the flat of your palm to experience nature. Be gentle, feel the back of a tree or the soft delicacy of flowers; then notice the difference.

A wonderful way to open up to touching with "new" hands is a Blind Walk, an exercise students and I have done together over the past 20 years. You need to enlist the help of a trusted friend, or perhaps another writer.

Blind Walk:

Two people pair up: Partner "A" puts on a blind-fold and Partner "B" leads that person by the arm through a garden or some safe place, where they can only "see" using their hands, or senses of smell or hearing. The guide must commit to being mindful of the "blind" partner's steps, as well as her hands, during the walk. After 20 minutes or so, the partners switch: Partner "B" puts on the blindfold and is then led by Partner "A." Afterwards, both people write about their experiences.

The writing that comes from this exercise is amazing. It's also a wonderful way to learn about your surroundings. Writer Within loves this, as your power of expression truly expands. (Your lover might enjoy it too.)

An example of some writing after a blind walk is...

Touch the tendrils of the night as she lets down her silken tresses into my hands; hands that savor her face, as I would my grandmother's, rough and wrinkled, like the bark of an old cedar tree, smelling pungent; her scent fills my nasal cavity. My fingers want to explore her skin, have her talk to me in the sounds of a breeze.

From the perspective of person "B" who walked her partner...

At first, unsure, timidly inching her way across the soft damp grass, she clings to my arm, nervous, wondered, perplexed.

Then, bending down, she touches delicate pink blossoms, makes love to them, caressing, stroking her cheek with one sweet petal. Soon, she is more certain; this blossom is her friend now, her lover.

We walk; she removes her navy blue shoes; smiles as the grass tickles her feet.

We move to the holly trees; she explores; in-between the prickled edges; the young green shoots satiny smooth; no need for hard protection yet.

Now, a wide grin crinkles her face as a breeze ruffles her hair.

I watch as she fondles a Hemlock tree trunk, like her man's firm body, exploring, tendering; her tentative touching turns to trust.

Later, she touches the Elm, palming its recent wound

It is only rough on the outside; inside it bleeds sap.

I recall Alice Cooper's song, "only women bleed." No, trees do, too.

I thrill to witness this woman, blind, evolving into a gleeful little child. Time doesn't exist, but the world and this woman/child seem more real.

(c) Taste in New Ways:

Your lover would probably be delighted to have you experiment with new tastes – such as arms, ears or... (hey, let your imagination run wild)! So would your Writer Within...

Lick things, savor them. When you eat, don't just gulp and swallow, but really taste: Is it sweet or sour, pungent or musky, bitter or surprisingly savory? Put a (non-poisonous!) flower in your mouth. Press your tongue against a piece of wood. Notice the difference. This opens your senses, so you can appreciate more of your world. In doing this, your Writer Within is expanded and opened - so she can actually write about more of the world.

(d) Stimulate Your Sense of Smell:

Why do we wear perfumes or after-shave lotions for our partners? Those expensive scents stimulate all of our senses, and hopefully, draw our lover closer.

Many scents stimulate us – and our Writer Within: the smell of freshly-mown lawn; concrete pavement after a hard rain; freshly-squeezed orange juice; rubbing a sprig of cedar between your fingers; or the scent of a bonfire on the beach. These words describe just a few scents familiar to you, but no doubt you have noticed already that even in memory, the sense of smell can transport a reader faster to the scene than any other of our five senses.

So, when you sit down to write, inhale deeper and include the many scents in your story: i.e. the aroma of coffee; the fragrance of a rose on your table; the fishy-salty smell in the ocean air; or the stench of tar being poured onto the pavement – it can soothe your soul, or spoil your mood. Pay more attention to the smells around you, be they sweet fragrances or foul odors, and you'll have more to write about.

You will open up your Writer Within in new ways to enrich her life, and your own. Your readers will be breathing deeply too as they are engaged by the scents that draw them in readily. When you encourage your sensuality you will be reawakening your passion.

Chapter 41. Keep The Sparks Lit

Maintain your curiosity about life and you will be a more interesting person – within, or without a relationship. In midlife, we often get into ruts, don't we? It's true; our habitual ways of living can block our flow of creativity. So we need to be attentive to what would open us to new ways of living and playing and being in our lives.

When you decide to keep the sparks lit in relationship to your lover – and your Writer Within – you'll literally see new things and make new connections between them. Hey, you just might have fun too!

Do things differently than you usually do:

Walk a different way home, whether you're on your way to your house, or venturing out for your daily constitutional. Eat a new fruit – like kiwi, which is a very pretty picture on a plate, or an Asian ly chee "nut," which hides an explosion of soft, cool freshness inside its rough, homely skin. Change one daily habit - like, swim earlier or go to a different pool. These little changes will ignite your curiosity, which in turn fosters your creativity and helps sustain the relationship with your Writer within.

Nurture in Nature:

Lovers walk in the park holding hands. Nature nurtures greater loving closeness with all that is around us. So, make it a habit to sustain your Writer Within this way.

Write through (that is, *become*) a tree or a character you see walking on the street. Do the same exercise as you did inside your home (chapter 32). Fall in love with the tree or that person on the street (of course you don't have to tell them!). Study the object, or that person, then close your eyes and write through them. This is the way to write very interesting characters – and the process will surprise and delight you.

Maybe you never even thought of yourself as a "fiction" writer. But your characters could be the beginning of a great creative project. For instance, the animation market is growing and your characters could be developed into a film script. You never know! Try it. Your Writer Within will enjoy this because the experience not only enhances your sense of sight, it also awakens your insight.

Visit Out-of-the-way places:

Just as your lover would enjoy a new little bistro or outdoor café, so will your Creative Self. She will be titillated with your romancing, and as long as you have your notebook, new places like these with new people to watch, that new atmosphere with the aromatic scent of coffee will stimulate your writing. Relaxed as you sip your latte and open your notebook, you will open up and write more easily.

Do what excites you:

Write what you love to write! For example, if writing songs turns you on, then write them. Get the microphone ready, hang out at songwriter's gatherings, jazz yourself with this environment. Get the guitar fixed, repair strings; replace them with silk ones. Take lessons if you have to – and trust that if you really feel excited by music and songwriting, then you are being led by your Writer Within. When you're smiling, Writer Within is smiling too.

My friend, Keith, has suddenly become turned on by Bram Stoker and now wants to write Gothic stories, because he is excited by what that author does with his stories; when you walk through the forest in a Bram Stoker novel, the trees seem to actually be growing – and other such romantic, fantastical details. Keith loves these stories on the wild side, and listening to him, I heard his renewed excitement and passion about his writing.

Keep a list of all the things that excite you in your life, such as...

* Being out in a sailboat on a beautiful sunny day.

* Dancing in your most beautiful red dress like a wild woman.

* Playing silly games with your friends.

* Attending Bruce Springsteen concerts.

* Exploring a brand new little village.

* Flying off to someplace new.

* Reading your poetry at an open-mic night.

* Eating ice-cream with chocolate sauce slathered on it – for breakfast.

* Sleeping in a hotel with your partner – even if you've been together for years.

* Ordering room-service.

* Luxuriating in a Jacuzzi in a beautiful setting.

* Treating your body to a massage.

* Hopping on a local ferry – not to get anywhere, but just to ride on the water.

* Taking mini-trips within your own city.

* Going to a comedy club.

* Enrolling in a Toastmaster's group and giving speeches.

* Hosting creativity "salons," where everybody gets to perform.

* Laughing a lot!

Take a Day Off:

Oh boy, a mini-vacation! Don't we all need these? Your lover will love some relaxing, nothing-on-the-agenda time together with you. And just as you would make time for your lover, your Writer Within will delight in time off. A day to loosen up the logic will keep the sparks lit, and open you up to a greater stream of writing the next day

You may experience guilt or annoyance when you even think of taking a day off. In our culture of fast-paced living, of accomplishing all that we were meant to do, we forget that our body and soul need rest and relaxation in order to function at maximum efficiency. But if we don't take a day off, often the only way we get a rest is if we finally get the flu or something worse. Better to take the time off – before that happens.

Goof off. Do not think. Sleep. Chill out. Walk. Go to a movie - or two. Take a sensual bath with candles. Doodle. Go shopping - try Value Village; treat yourself. If you're sleepy, take a nap. Don't be such a slave-driver!

Clarissa Pinkola Estes reminds us in her book *Women Who Run with the Wolves*, "If we were to abuse our children, Social Services would show up at our doors. If we were to abuse our pets, the Humane Society would come to take us away. But there is no Creativity Patrol or Soul Police to intervene if we insist on starving our own souls." [72]

I realized that my soul was indeed hungry – for ease, rest, goofing off – so I followed my own advice yesterday. Today, the fog has disappeared from my overloaded brain, my mind is clearer, and I hear Writer Within whispering, *"Thank you, thank you. Let's do this again soon."*

Keeping the sparks lit in different ways reawakens your passion and your writing starts to feel brand new.

Chapter 42. Ask: What Opens Your Heart Wider?

If you ask this question, answer it and then, actually do what opens your heart wider, you will become more available to relationship with your lover.

Your Writer Within will also receive your clear intention that you are willing to expand and write at a deeper level. For example:

Visit a Seniors' Residence: Our elders are like walking libraries of history and adventure, and to let them tell their stories is to be transported to times and places we could otherwise never know. If you've ever enjoyed this experience with the elders in your own extended family, you know how it can open your heart. Consider going to a local seniors' centre or residence, and ask if anyone wants to record his/her stories. If so, commit to one person for two months or so. Go once a week, sit, listen and record the elder's stories. Type them up at home, and create a small book for that person's family. You will be more inspired to tell your own stories.

I did this over some months for a dear old friend of mine named Nigel. I was very moved by his tears as he expressed stories he had never before revealed. One was about a near-fatal plane crash, and he just sobbed as he told it to me. Later, at his funeral, his son said to me, *"I'm so glad you wrote up my Dad's stories. I read one every night, and I know him a lot better now."*

I was honored to spend time with him in this process. It not only resulted in a book for him to gift his friends with on his 80th birthday, but it opened my heart wider than I ever expected. In hindsight, I also see how deeply I engaged with my Writer Within to produce such a special piece of work.

Ask yourself what ways might open your heart wider. Here are some are suggestions:

Choose Good Music: I love listening to classical music, and sometimes I just have to stop what I'm doing and listen to the whole piece. One of my favorites is Rachmaninoff's Concerto in C# minor, which he wrote after his clinical depression forced him to a hypnotherapist, who helped him through his creative wall. Every time I hear this piece, I know that if he could write such amazing music, directly from his soul, then maybe I could also venture deeper into my writing.

Early in my marriage, I experienced depression too; so I would turn up the volume on this piece so loudly that my then-husband, walking home from public transit, could hear it two blocks away. (Everybody must've heard it too.) Public nuisance notwithstanding, that piece always opens my heart, and now as I even think of that earlier time, I smile and remember the young woman in her twenties who was struggling to stay sane and grounded for her two little children, in a challenging marriage. That music helped keep her heart open. What are your favorites? Do you play them and really listen?

Watch Films: Alfred Hitchcock always said of the film business that it was *"the e-motion picture business."* He always believed that films should move our emotions; if not, what's the point of paying your money, sitting through two hours, and not feeling something? If you want a good cry – you know, when you're on this side of a cry but it just won't happen– then watch *The Bridges Of Madison County*, or *Out of Africa*. Recently, I saw *Mao's Last Dancer*, which was inspirational, and I'll never forget *Rainman*, or *Tootsie*. Make a list of your films that touch you, or make you laugh out loud – then watch them!

View Art: Go to the art gallery in your city, and be in awe at some of the Master's work. This will open your heart wider. Years ago, when my family was in London England, we went to the British Museum of Art, and my eight-year-old daughter was so moved by a Turner painting that she said, "Oh Mom, can't you just hear the wind?" Immediately, we bought her a drawing pad and colored pencils. Buy your own paper and acrylic paints and just see what you can do with them. You'll be surprised.

Call a loved one long distance and get caught up: Let that person know you were just thinking of her/him and wanted to reach out. Say, *"I love you,"* and mean it. When we share love, we feel love our within us – and the remembrance enriches us. Isn't that the most important thing in our lives?

Read a good book: Browse in a book store. Used book stores are exciting too because they have the smells of old books, and that can trigger old feelings and open your heart. Allow yourself to sit and read pages from whatever book attracts you. Read poetry if you don't usually. Or an author you have heard of but have never read. Go to your community library, feel the bustle there from other curious people, and you'll be reminded that you are not alone in your literary ventures.

Give of Yourself: Drive to your friend's home and help her/him unpack boxes. Help out at your church or community center. Read to a shut-in. Take soup to a new mother who has no time for herself. Offer to babysit. Create a newsletter in your apartment building. Offer to read your friend's manuscript and give her/him a gentle critique; every writer needs a person like this in her life. Make phone calls for your community project. Offer yourself up. Oprah has always said that she prayed: *"Use me, God."* And we all know what wonderful work she is doing. If you don't know how you can be used as an instrument of the divine, then pray for an answer. Doing so will open your heart much wider.

Your Writer Within will be delighted with any of these ideas you try out.

Chapter 43. Remember Miracles

Can you remember some amazing times when mystery seemed to rule, and you experienced bliss beyond understanding? There was no other explanation for what occurred than to say, *"It was a miracle!"* Talking about it, we rise up, just recalling that experience. When we share these miracles with our lover, we get it that we are not living our lives alone. And our bond together grows tighter – feeling merged within a deep sense of spirituality.

Similarly, with our Writer Within, as we recall and write our miracles, we are lifted up to a higher realm, and we know that divine Self and I are one. Must be.

So, with those thoughts in mind, I want to share one of the miracles I've experienced in my life. As you read, I invite you to remember that blessings come in many forms, and they always expand love.

This miracle happened many years ago, when my son David was just fourteen. He'd bought a dirt bike, a Yamaha 100; not very big, but powerful enough to be dangerous. He'd badgered me about having one, and finally I'd said, "Only if you buy it with your own money" – thinking, *how is he going to get that?* Of course, his power of intention was working overtime, and through working as a janitor for his uncle's company that summer, he earned enough to purchase it. He'd only had it about a week when I received that bloodcurdling call: *Mrs. Burns, your son has been in an accident so you'd better get over here.*

Shakily, I drove to the hill, just off Yosemite Street in Denver, where lots of kids revved up their motorcycles, and there was an unwritten rule: *You can zoom up this dirt hill but you never ride down it.* A new boy did not know those rules. That kid drove a *250 Kawasaki,* a much larger bike and he was zooming downhill while David was zooming up fast – to make the jump at the top of the hill. Just as he was about to make an "amazing jump" his leg collided with the other boy's motorcycle – nearly ripping it off.

In the ambulance, my son reached for my hand – something he had not done for years – so I knew something *must* be really bad. The paramedics had attended to him before I got there, and "casted" his whole leg in a plastic balloon-type apparatus, so neither of us actually saw how serious the injury was – only that he was now in shock, shivering and scared witless.

In the emergency room, I was horrified to witness a doctor inserting a huge needle into David's belly, to check for internal bleeding I suppose, and as I was obviously squeamish about this, a nurse guided me to a chair in the waiting room. My neighbor and friend, Merilane, met me at the hospital, Swedish General, and kindly sat there through the long vigil, well into the early morning hours, to wait with me.

It was 1.30 a.m. before a doctor came out and called me over to where he stood with a clip-board in hand. He exuded an attitude of ultra-authority, I-am-King-Doctor-here-so-you'd-better-listen, and he said: *"Your son has severe injuries to his leg, it is hanging on only by the Achilles tendon and the only thing we can do is to amputate. So, sign here, will you?"*

My legs buckled a bit and I nearly fell over, but a beige wall caught me. All I could think was: This can't be happening to my natural-athlete son – how will he play hockey and tennis? – how will he live a normal life without his leg? There has to be something better than this... So, the mother-hen voice muttered, *"No, I will not sign."*

"Mrs. Burns, I don't think you heard me correctly. The leg is filled with dirt and pebbles and cannot be saved, so if you don't sign, he may develop gangrene and it will be worse."

I stood up strongly then, more like a cocky rooster, faced this good-looking dude, looked him square in his grey eyes, and said, *"No. No. No, I won't sign. Fix it."*

You can imagine the stunned look on his face; his eyebrows rose up high, his glasses fell down onto his perfectly straight nose, his mouth was agape, and then his lips pressed together tightly in anger as he shook his head at me. *"You're making a huge mistake."*

"Please fix it."

So, the doctor walked away, and I learned later that what he and his team did was to clean out the pebbles, sand and dirt; jam the splintered leg bones together in a semblance of how it should be; and put a plaster cast on it. Then, David was wheeled into a hospital room upstairs. When I finally got to see him, he looked so little, and so groggy – but there was his leg, in one "apparent" piece. So, I never told him how bad it was. Never mentioned that the newspapers had reported: "In a dirt-bike accident, a young fellow has had his leg torn right off." No, as far as he could see, his leg was right there in front of him, in a plaster cast, hoisted up on pillows.

Driving home with Merilane, she asked if I would like her to form a prayer chain. I said, *"What's that?"* She, who was a fundamental Baptist church-goer, informed me that many people would pray for David around the clock. Naturally, I agreed. It couldn't hurt!

The accident happened September 26th, so for each day of the following two weeks, I would visit my son; sometimes I'd wash his hair (very gently and tenderly in a basin placed at the back of his head which was propped up with pillows) and other times I just sat beside him and we'd talk, or be quiet together. His father came to visit from Calgary, so David knew that this must be a serious injury, but still, he never knew that he could lose his leg – only that it was propped up like he expected it to be – there in that white cast (now oozing yellow gunk). So it must be in one piece.

On October 13th, the Canadian Thanksgiving Day, David's big toe moved! This was huge. How did it happen? We were overjoyed. The doctors were gob-smacked! Yes, it looked like David might have a leg to stand on after all. This was a miracle!

Gradually, after six further operations, David began to heal – and by the following September he was actually playing tennis on the Tennis Team at his high school. A miracle indeed!

On one of our last visits with David's orthopedic surgeon, he said, *"My partner and I do not know how your son still has his leg... His was an impossible case. We'd never seen one so bad. Normally, that leg would have been amputated."*

I said, *"It must have been the power of prayer."*

Apparently, that doctor was going to write the case up in a medical journal.

And as I write this today, I still tear up because I know it was God-in-action. Two specialists were unable to "fix" that leg – but Divine Universal Energy did. So, I believe in miracles – that is for sure! And I am reminded how wonderful they are. And how small we are in relation to what is possible!

Thus, with our writing, miracles can happen there, too – anywhere!

May this story trigger your memory about your own miracles. Doing so will reawaken your passion to write.

Chapter 44. Take Her To A Writer's Circle

When your lover truly sees who you are, you can more readily expand and grow in his/her presence. With your writing, you will be fostering your creativity when you're in the company of others who see who you are. As Rumi says, this will "help your being." He writes about how important it is for us to associate with those who see who we truly are:

> *Be with those who help your being*
> *Don't sit with indifferent people,*
> *Whose breath comes cold out of their mouths.*
> *Not these visible forms, your work*
> *Is deeper...*
> *Rumi, Ode 2865* [73]

Joining a writer's circle will "help your being." Jean Shinoda Bolen writes about how, in sharing within a group of other women, one's oxytocin (the "hormone of love") levels physically rise. [74] Circles of women writers, who see you and hear you, can lift your consciousness and remind you that you belong.

For the past twenty years I have witnessed this phenomenon in the writing groups I lead. The women read their pieces, nervously at first; and then, after they finish, they await the group's feedback – which, in these groups, is always non-judgmental. We do our very best to find phrases, or rhythms or words or sentences that have moved us, and we speak about that. Of course, the writer is mostly always glowing, because they have not only written a piece that might initially have been challenging to write, but they are delighted with their own creative expression. One can nearly feel that oxytocin rising! There is definitely love in the room.

Some exercises include: Giving some opening lines or pictures from a magazine, and the writers are then told to write quickly, say for ten minutes or less. Sometimes, this might include another five minutes of clustering on ideas. But often, the writers just put pen to the page and witness what comes through. I remind them that some famous writers do write that way, not knowing where they are going, but simply writing and not thinking about it. This is the most exciting aspect of creativity: you are putting your pen on the page and your Writer Within seems to be writing the piece, for surely, you are not in control! Afterwards, upon looking at it and reading it aloud, you will be quite amazed to hear your own piece. In every session with students, I get to witness shiny eyes, huge smiles – and awe.

Whatever writing group you join, make sure it is non-critical – because it will shut your creativity right down if you are judged, analyzed or criticized in any way. There is a time and place for constructive feedback, and for considering revisions. However, I believe that a writing group, where you hope to develop your creativity, is not the place to get "corrected." In Chapter 7 we discussed the rules of brainstorming; those are, in a sense, guidelines for enhancing your creative powers. Positive feedback, and no criticism, is crucial when your work is in its formative stages.

Imagine you've just given birth to a brand new baby and some "expert" is trying to prove how smart, or advanced, or sophisticated he or she is, saying: *"Well, the ears are sure sticking out, aren't they? And what a flat head that child has. He's not very cute."* Of course, you would not put your beautiful baby in that person's arms anymore; you'd stay as far away from him/her as possible. It is the same thing with our brand new baby creations: when they are that new they do not deserve criticism – only acknowledgment that the piece emerged from you!

A writing group needs to be supportive, encouraging and loving so that you and your Writer Within feel safe. Creativity within a writing group only thrives in an environment of psychological safety, so seek that in your chosen group if you want to truly move ahead in your writing. Good groups should instill confidence within you and through that, your passion will awaken. Trust your own instincts in this regard.

I remember, with distaste and a pain in my stomach, when I took a songwriting class in Los Angeles, in a boiling hot seminar room, must've been 100 degrees in there; near Sunset and Vine, right in the middle of Hollywood. When asked to play my new song, I stumbled over to the old upright piano, sat down, set my music book on the piano, and with sweat pouring down my sides, put my fingers on the keys. While trying to hit some of the right chords, I attempted to sing at the same time. Not my forte! Flashbacks to the recital I gave when I was 12, when I flubbed the first few bars of Liebestraum and my father was in that audience and I was sweating in my taffeta dress... I quit my classical studies in music after that. Now, here I was in this dinky little room in Hollywood, having smashed and clashed my way through my song. The teacher said, *"Well now... okay, you tried... but I don't think that was very good, do you?"* The rest of the group snickered, and looked away. I desperately wanted to hide my flaming face, and wished with all my heart that a trap door would open and I'd fall through to a whole new world!

After that experience, I didn't write songs for a whole year. See, when we are thoughtlessly judged the door to our creativity slams shut pretty quickly.

Be kind to your Creative Self and put her into environments that support and sustain that creative expression. When you do, you will be reawakening your passion, which you will find very exciting!

Chapter 45. Show How You Believe In Her

This story demonstrates that we need both the feminine Inner Self to write, and the masculine aspect to take action. Full creativity takes both. Just as in a relationship with our lover, we often need to be both "mother" and "father," or "sister" and "brother." Any full human being comprises both masculine and feminine. I hope that this story motivates you to take action on something you've written.

It's about visualization, belief in self - and belief in Creative Self:

When I was writing my dissertation, the chairman of my committee never approved any of the six drafts I'd written for Chapter One and I was starting to think that while I'd end up with a Ph.D., I'd be insane! So, what did I do? I wrote a film script to take my mind off the academic stuff.

Yep, there I was, perched on the edge of my couch, back straight, for fear I'd lose the idea (which felt like a dream) and wrote out the whole story for a film script, in about an hour or so. It was about a woman who leaves her mid-western home, her husband, and takes off for California, where she *finds* herself. I worked day and night and finished the script within a week; yes, I was driven. I had to do it!

In-between the writing, trying to sleep, *I would lie in my bed and visualize handing this script to Jane Fonda* - the most powerful woman I knew of in movies. I saw us meeting in a supermarket, where I would walk up to her, talk to her, then reach into my purse and present my script to her. Three weeks later, I did just that! How? Well, it took INTENTION, DESIRE, and SEEING it clearly in my mind.

While staying in L.A. with a friend, I saw in a magazine that Jane Fonda would be speaking to the Lawyers' Wives of America at the Beverly Hilton Hotel. So I went! I wasn't going to miss this opportunity!

I must've looked pretty different than most of the "lawyers' wives" because I wasn't wearing diamond earrings, didn't have long red nails, didn't own a designer suit and knew not a soul. However, dressed in my very simple outfit and armed with my script in my handbag, I paid my registration fee and entered the huge ballroom of this grand hotel. As luck would have it, I was seated with a lovely lawyer's mother in her 60's, a most supportive woman.

Ms. Fonda spoke. I listened raptly. Her speech enthralled me, as she spoke about a woman's strength and how each one of us could make a contribution. I seemed to be the only one listening: many of the women were chatting amongst themselves and the room was abuzz with rudeness. Too soon, Jane wrapped up her remarks, and with the applause billowing around me, I watched her exit Stage Left – while I was sitting way, way over, close to Stage Right. For a moment, I shook my head and said to my table companion, *"I don't think I can reach her now."* But she said, *"Go for it! You came here to give her your script, so now it's up to you."*

Nodding my thanks to her, I strode across that huge chasm of a room, through pointy elbows and long flashing fingernails, *"Excuse me, excuse me... oops, sorry,"* as I stepped on a few bare toes – until finally, I reached the enormous gold curtain where Jane had exited.

Boldly, I peeked through it, saw that she was still there, with her back to me. But facing us both was a battery of photographers. *Well, I don't know you and you don't know me*, I muttered under my breath, then, brazenly I stepped into the inner sanctum.

Quietly, so as not to startle her: *"Ahem, excuse me Ms. Fonda, may I speak with you before you leave?"* She turned towards me, and with great charm shining through her porcelain skin, she said, *"Well, I have to leave right now."*

So, I glanced at the impatient photographers, whose photo-op I had just interrupted, and shrugged my shoulders; it was now or never. *"I have a script here that pertains to everything you just spoke about, so would you read it?"*

She asked, *"Is it registered and copyrighted?"* I nodded, *"Yes, of course."* So, with a smile on her face, she took it and shook my hand. A paparazzo came and placed my script on the carpet. But Jane reached down, picked it up and clasped it to her bosom – so my script was photographed with her. Oh, what a moment!

Less than one year later, I moved out to Los Angeles with my three teenaged children. No, Jane Fonda's company did not do the film, but that action proved to me that dreams can come true – that I didn't have to be a slave to an academic requirement. (Post-script: Five years later, I finished my dissertation from L.A. and was granted my Ph.D.)

In retrospect, I realized perhaps a greater lesson: that I should have visualized that script emblazoned on the theater billboard! So, when you are visualizing, SEE THE RESULTS YOU DESIRE FULLY. Don't stop half-way.

Be kind to your Writer Within and steward your work. Then, the communion with Creative Self will continue to grow.

Chapter 46. Converse With Her

All partners need to sit down, face to face, to discuss issues directly to strengthen their relationship – which, by midlife, you probably realize.

You can do this with your Writer Within. How? By closing your eyes for a few moments, taking several deep breaths, then asking a question of her.

For example: I did this very exercise the other day, related to the insomnia I'd had the night before, when I was lying awake till 4 in the morning. Very frustrating. Here's how the dialogue with my Creative Self went...

...Jaya, please speak to me about why a person doesn't sleep well, even though they are tired out and their body craves sleep...

Dear One, Is it possible that you may only be listening to that which you want to hear during the daytime? At night, the soul calls loudly because it has important things to tell you. Do not despair, for these feelings are to heal you; they are important to your longing soul. Allow. You will gain from this experience. When you do not fight these feelings, your inner conflicts wave the white flag of truce.

Okay, but I still don't like the insomnia.

Your sleeplessness is a message to you, is it not?

I guess so.

Yes, it may be informing you to take more quiet time during the day, to allow your heart to catch up to your mind. Just as the sea tosses and churns from undercurrents meeting outer currents of wind and air pressure, so its waves are high. Other times, that sea is calm and glistening. In nature, both/all are important to the balance, and you do not judge them - except when your boat is riding those waves. If you can remain above it all, the power of you remains still; still present, omnipresent. Do not judge your sleepless nights, just ride them out, up and down, and learn from them.

I feel so frustrated though, watching that darned clock move further and further into morning time.

When your mind goes to all the old thoughts in the middle of the night, realize that you are given a gift of vulnerability and tiredness, so you can see some old thoughts that you need to bring to consciousness. Bless them, for they are brought to the light then, and you can choose whether or not to let them go. Trust the tossing and turning and breathe into it. <u>Breath is the key</u>. *Breathe deeply and feel the gift of oxygen filling you, and you will feel more peaceful. Would you even have an instant of doubt that I am not here with you? I am here with you in the middle of the night as you wonder why you are here.*

Have you ever pondered such deep questions during the hours of light? Or do you fill up your days with so much busyness you do not take time to let your soul speak? Is it any wonder that you need the time in the wee hours of the night to do that?

Hmmm, I'm beginning to "get" what you mean.

Trust that your life force needs to speak with you. Take the time to listen. Then, during the daylight hours, stay in the NOW. Read some of your own writing. See what gifts you've been given. Open up to the energy flowing through you. Trust that you are guided always. You have work to do and you are doing it. First, you must pause and be still. Be gentle this day. Eat right, exercise, be kind, be slow, and trust that your work is going well. All is perfect really, isn't it?

I suppose it is, even if I'm tired. I sure can't rush around too much.

Stay in the present moment, breathe in deeply to the feeling of peace within, and you will live a more fully conscious and peaceful life.

I can feel it – and I'm so grateful for these dialogues Jaya.

Share this with your readers and it will open doorways, so that writers may learn how to dialogue with their Creative Selves.

Thank you. I will.

Therefore, I have chosen to share this dialogue with that intention – to open your heart and connect it directly with your pen on the paper. Perhaps then you won't just tell your stories, but you will write them from your heart and soul – always with your Writer Within guiding you.

Trust that you have this ultimate communication with your Writer Within, and that when you become more conscious of it, you will remember that you are not writing all alone.

Just as every crisis offers an opportunity for action that can bring about good, the angst of middle age need not be labeled 'bad' just because it's painful or uncomfortable. It is emotional energy, and what matters is what we do with it.
Dr. Gene D. Cohen [75]

Chapter 47. Ask For Her Help

In relationship with your partner, you probably take each other into confidence about what you are each trying to do in your life. Sometimes, you will ask for support, say, in the writing of a book or any form of creating; you may ask him/her to tune in with your dream and show you how important it is to them too. In this kind of sharing, closeness develops.

In writing with your Writer Within, you can also ask for help. I know that I have done so, in the writing of this book and many others. There were times I felt stymied, but would meditate and ask for guidance – and it always came. I trust that process deeply now. I am not a person who easily asks other people for help – but I can confidently ask my Creative Self, and when I do, I find my heart opening.

Here is an example of my request for help from Jaya...

Ask For Her Help

Dear Jaya, I am so grateful for your presence, and I know that you have gotten me through so many situations and difficulties, and loneliness too. Thank you. Now, is there anything I am not seeing this book. Anything I really need to put into it?

Dear one, Perhaps you have overlooked the very things that you take for granted – such as journaling, and having your Writer Within be your friend and confidante. And your notebook can be (to paraphrase Charles Dickins in A Tale of Two Cities), for "the best of times and the worst of times." In it, you can write about your empty nest and your fears, or your "age of wisdom" or your "age of foolishness," and through doing so, rise above them. It is I who lead you through the valley of the shadow, where you get to fear not, but know you are guided gently and kindly to look at situations in new ways. For example, when one of your children turned their back on you, you had Me, your Wise self, and did that not lift you up from the darkness? Knowing that I am always with you, does that not soothe you?

Yes, you always bring me a sense of calm.

So, allow me to truly co-author your book. Please step out of the way when you ask for guidance, and allow my wisdom to come through. Just as you are doing this very moment, could this not be one of the chapters in your book? ASK FOR HELP. You will inevitably receive it quickly.

You're saying that I can ask and pray to you and you will truly be there for me – even to help me write a book?

Yes. Remember, I am perpetually within you, a silver thread in the fabric of you; a constant note in your tonality; a life force that lifts your head up high. Trust that I am always with you. And I love you.

Thank you Jaya. So, I have a question about whether or not I should include a personally revealing story in this book – or if it would be better in another book I'm writing?

Trust your feelings. If you are experiencing doubt about this point, recall how your printer suddenly went out of commission today and you were unable to print your book. Do you think that was an accident?

Probably not. Earlier, I was close to tears. Now, I smile as I think about it.

Again, trust those feelings. You needed to ponder this. You needed to honor your self - your Self.

Okay, I get it. I shall not rush this through. Perhaps that particular story deserves a whole other place in a golden-penned book.

Feel the softness in your heart now from tuning in at a deeper level.

I feel it. Thank you.

So, you see, I have not written this book alone, but have partnered with my Creative Self. You can do the same. All you need to do is ask. Try it. It's a wonderful experience. As you dialogue with your Writer Within, observe how your passion reawakens.

Chapter 48. Make It A Habit To Romance Her

A healthy relationship will grow even stronger if each partner reminds the other that they're happy to be with each other: even in little ways, to show your loved one you care. Hold him/her close and say *"I love you."*

Make it a habit to romance your Writer Within too.

Buy yourself good tools for your writing, stand taller, walk with vigor, write encouraging words to her on a regular basis and demonstrate that you care greatly about your Writer Within. You will begin to sense the deep connection with her. Your Writer Within will come through as a Quiet Presence more often, and when you acknowledge how much you love her, you will feel that love within you.

When you improve your habits towards this writer in you, your attitude will naturally become more positive. And with this energy, your writing will take on new life! Make it a habit to woo your Creative Self and the love between you will continue to grow.

Now that you have wooed and wed, just like a good marriage, it is important to sustain this relationship and always honor it.

*Here are some ways to sustain your relationship and continue to **make it a habit** to romance your Writer Within:*

1. Persevere:

All relationships take perseverance; otherwise, you would catapult from one to another, never having worked out your own individual issues. Your writing takes perseverance too. No one can take it away from you; no one owns your work, your task, as you do. You get to decide. If you quit, you'll fail. But if you sit your bottom down in the chair, quietly persist as you pick up your pen and press it from your heart onto the page, you will arrive at your destination: a finished product, a work of art, a book, a completed plan to guide you home. Your life is yours. Listen to the words your soul speaks directly to you. Hope isn't enough – that is, just hoping you'll get to where you're going without putting your Self into it. Persist.

Tony Robbins, in his book *Awaken the Giant Within*, says of persistence: "In fact, in studying the source of people's success, I've found that persistence overshadows even talent as the most valued and effective resource in creating and shaping the quality of life. Most people give up a maddening five feet from their goal." [76]

What does it take to persist and persevere? *Discipline.*

Discipline is that old-fashioned concept whereby you decide to do something, intend that you will – and then carve out of your life those hours you need to do it. When you do this, the universe knows that you are serious. Books get done this way – people evolve and change this way: being like a pit bull with a stick in its mouth, never letting go. Writing every day. Trusting you can do it – and will. No one can take it away from you!

2. *Send out your writings:*

Don't you enjoy showing off your lover? Parading arm in arm, walking out together demonstrates that you are proud to be with this person.

Likewise with your finished pieces of writing, demonstrate that you are proud of them, too. Send them out. Even if they are sent back to you, send them anyway.

If necessary, create a blog so you know that somebody is reading them. Keep on going. Don't give in to the temptation (like I often did) to keep them in your filing cabinets and "get around to it" eventually. Keep on sending them out. They will be published.

3. Remember the Golden Rule:

We learn the Golden Rule that says to love thy neighbor as thyself –but we must also learn to *"Love thyself as thy neighbor."* This applies to your relationships as well as to your Writer Within.

Be supportive of your own writing and trust that if you want to write, you can. Practice it. Give it time and energy. Don't judge it. Just as you would not want to be judged by your partner, do not judge what comes onto the page.

Love yourself and love your Writer Within. Doing so will create a habit of kindness, and your writing will flow – past all those old blocks, past your resistance on any day, past your self-sabotage. You will be surprised at what appears on the page.

Hold onto your dreams – like you'd hold the hand of a child.

4. Laugh a lot:

Don't you feel better after you've had a great laugh? Dr. Daniel Amen agrees: "A growing body of scientific literature suggests that laughter counteracts stress and is good for the immune system... Laugher can lower blood pressure, trigger a flood of endorphins (the brain chemicals that can bring on euphoria and decrease pain) and enhance our immune systems..." [77] He reminds us that an average child has great fun and laughs at least hundreds of times a day. But the average adult only laughs about 12 times per day. Poetically, he suggests, "If only we could collect those lost laughs and use them to our advantage." [78]

So, do things that make you laugh, see funny movies, read those silly jokes on the internet and send them out, whatever gives you a good belly laugh. It will open your brain and relax you; it's true, you will have a better brain to write with! And your Writer Within will love it that she is so much more available to you.

5. Remember that your creativity is ageless:

Remember, no matter how old you are, emotionally or chronologically, you can still write. When Barbara Cartland, the British "Queen of Romance" novels was

82, she entered the Guinness Book of Records for writing twenty-six books for one year, 1983. Her publishers estimated that since her writing career began in 1923 (when she was 22 years old), Cartland had produced 723 titles. She died when she was 98. [79]

When my dear mentor/friend, Fred Cogswell, was on his last trip to the hospital, where he passed away at 86, he insisted that his daughter, Kathleen, stop and put his last poetry-manuscript in the mail. It was his 48th book.

Creativity is ageless. Several of my writing students began when they were in their late fifties, and now, inching into their seventies, they are still writing books.

As you get into a project, be it a book of your essays, memoirs, short stories, a novel or a book of your poetry, the writing will lift you up and carry you forward in ways that restore your confidence, and fly you above the mundane. You will radiate passion and emanate aliveness.

When you recognize how crucial your creativity is, you will have more of yourself to give to others. You'll feel happier, laugh more, and live in wonder. So, make the time and the quiet, and with pen and paper in hand, express what wants to come through you! Doing so will align you with your Creative Self, your Writer Within – and you'll get to know what romance really is! Your courtship with you. Your loving ongoing relationship with you. It is Love.

Make it a habit to romance your Writer Within and your life will change.

When we commit to living the light of our spiritual potential, our 'golden' years will glow with fulfillment.
Diane Vilas [80]

Chapter 49. Commune With Her

My mother used to say, *"I don't know what I'm thinking 'til I hear myself say it."* That is a wise statement. We don't know what wants to come forth until we see it on a page. So, writing can open an ultimate communion with the Self. It is holy. It is a Love letter – even if old negativity emerges. It is sacred. And it will empower you to contribute to the world.

I asked my Writer Within to express more about writing, and this is what came out...

> *To not write is to turn your back on Self – To split off from the Essential Rock of Life.*
>
> *To write is to call forth, as if from one mountain top across a huge canyon, to another mountain top – which enables those separate selves to join and hear each other's words and feelings and intentions. It is to bring forth Oneness and to*

honor that Greatness. Writing can give you a sense of awe as you tap into Truth. Writing can soothe, or injure, the reader. It can inform, touch, open a heart - or shut it.

Writing can expand one's world by enabling your soul to speak. Writing gives voice to all those unspoken urges, impulsion; it is Life force. Like an infant birthing, writing comes out squalling and pink and slimy; wondrously beautiful! It is a silver thread connecting each fragment of self with the Greater Soul. It reconnects you with your TRUE self.

And so I get *it*: Creativity is a golden filament connecting us to the Divine. It is precious, a treasure; a gift to honor. It connects you with your inner child. It merges you with your Greatness. It allows you to speak through others and to know them deeply. It makes new connections. It draws forth that which is pre-verbal and opens you to that lovely voice within. Through this loving relationship with your Writer Within, you will have a stronger foundation from which to bring your creativity out to the world:

> *The sacred Feminine is returning to the world through ordinary women who are carrying the healing power of the feminine and Goddess back into the world.*
> *Jean Shinoda Bolen* [81]

How might you carry this healing power of the feminine back into the world?

Ponder the old expression, *"The pen is mightier than the sword."* How might you use your writing? What are you passionate about? Express that passion in words, so people can read it and learn; so they are motivated to take action. Perhaps it means writing letters to the editor, or articles, or keeping a blog – or emailing important ideas to your friends.

Dr. Bolen speaks to the insight called *"an assignment,"* and how you may feel intuitively compelled to assist your community, or suffering women and children in other countries; to take a stand about something that tugs at every fiber of your being. "There are many assignments," she says. "Some may present themselves and require an immediate response. It may feel like an irrational impulse to say 'yes!' in a blink..." [82]

If you are aligned with your Creative Self; in integrity with your full self, you may wish to partake in a helping activity – when you feel that you are truly committed. "Each of us has only our allotted time to use as we choose, midlife comes quickly to let us know how fast the years will go by before our stint here is over." [83]

So write daily to heighten your relationship with Writer Within – so you can also use your words to empower people in your world to take action upon something meaningful. Your words may not only inspire others, but motivate them into sacred activism.

Yes, as we all know, the years do fly by, but you can choose to use each day. Your awakened passion to write can awaken your readers, too. Yes, as Writer Within wrote: *writing can expand one's world.* Let your passion to write expand your world.

In summing up, I asked my Writer Within: What about midlife and creativity and passion? What needs saying? I want you, dear reader, to benefit from this book and be motivated to return to your creativity. I want you to give it another chance, to open to your Creative Self and draw forth what is in there. So Jaya, dear Writer Within and Creative Inner Soul, what more is there to say?

> *That your chronological age does not count, for what is within has always been there. All you need to do is remember and draw from it. You are the same being at 50 or 60, or 40 or 70, as you were when skinny dipping at 10, or padding around the lake in your bare feet. You are. You are Love. And if you would see that, embrace this beloved Self, you would see that you are one and the same.*

What about passion? How does it awaken?

By opening your eyes and ears and nostrils and sense of touch to what is all around you. By living in wonder to the nuances of it - like the tiny sparrows on your balcony railing, to their fluttery wings and little peeping voices; to the salty sea air, or the differences in the air after rain, and those little puddles still inside the cracks on the sidewalk; and to those grand vistas of mountains; to realizing that you are part of the landscape and seascape; that you belong here and your voice is, at least, as important as the peep of the sparrow. Age does not matter.

But what about when I lose my glasses or forget a word, or ponder whether I've still got the grit and determination to go for my dreams – and will they really matter anyway?

You may misplace your new glasses while they sit atop your head, but as long as you look within your heart and dive deep into those crevices within, you will discover your unique You. The view within is your You Tube (so to speak), to mirror Love. Love for self. You are the Self, you are not separate. Trust that I will speak/write any time you ask, any time you put pen to paper - but all I ask, implore of you, is that you will not judge what flows onto the page - simply let it come.

Midlife is simply a resting point along your journey, a bench to sit upon for a few moments, to pause and ask yourself a few questions: Where am I going? What do I want? What matters? What do I love to do? What do I value? Then take the necessary time to honor these answers. Write about them. Write through the eyes of your mother or father. Who were they at this stage in your life? Then, open your heart to allow what is within to emerge.

Your creative expression is a gift. Open your eyes to it. And write - whatever comes out - be it gobbledygook, silly words, cut up phrases, images you had forgotten; even if it makes no sense at this time. But, like dreams, they will inform you who you are. Allow! Enjoy. Trust - that what you've always searched for is right inside, and if you tap into it, you will surprise yourself! You may be older now, but you can still give birth to something new. A shiny new you.

You may still be gestating your story, but be prepared to receive it - so that when it slides out all shiny and wet onto the page, you, great midwife, will catch it, and treasure it. Trust this process. Love yourself always.

Return to your creativity - and let it lead you back to communion with your self. With that, how can you ever be alone? You have your Self.

Chapter 50. Give Thanks For Your Loving Relationship

In our daily lives, gratitude is a key to well-being. Gratitude toward your partner will grow the relationship. Gratitude toward your children and your whole family will weave a loving thread throughout the tapestries of those relationships.

Gratitude toward your communion with your Writer Within will stimulate and expand your creativity.

A Course in Miracles says...
Today, let us be thankful. We have come to gentler pathways and to smoother roads. There is no thought of turning back, and no implacable resistance to the truth... you can well be grateful for your gains, which are far greater than you realize... Be glad today... [84]

Remember how important your Writer Within is to you, and open to her words. As you spend more quality time with her, you align with your Creative Self, which allows you to write from deep integrity. Moreover, as you encourage your inner Self to emerge, you develop a lasting relationship with Who You Truly Are.

Isn't it time to consider the amazing riches we possess?
Robert MacNeil [85]

...surely we are called to become more fully what we are, in simple service to the richness of the universe of possibilities.
James Hollis [86]

Create a Gratitude Journal. Write in it daily and remind yourself how wonderful your life is, and how grateful you are that you can indeed write. When you wake up, choose to see the good rather than the negative. When you give thanks for what you have, your attitude shifts and your life grows richer. You may be experiencing challenges or difficulties, but if you choose to see these as lessons for your soul, your life will take on new meaning.

If you write about your experiences – fictionalizing them or writing memoirs – you will be deepening your readers' lives, too. Remember all the books through the years from which you have learned and grown? Well, just like those authors who wrote from their own experiences, know that any particularly challenging situation you may face is great fodder for your next essay or book, and that your writing through it will touch others, too. *Be grateful for all of it.*

By being thankful, and by doing the work I suggest in this book, you will not only be romancing your Writer Within, you will be merging with her – *like a lover*. Within this partnership, just as within any loving relationship, your soul will expand and move you forward to new heights. You will realize that her power ... is your power.

Writing from that power can lead you to wonder and passion, where miracles happen. Be open to them. It is exhilarating. You can be lifted to places beyond the mundane, to loftier realms where you can sit atop a cloud and survey your life; where suddenly, everything that seemed to hold your heart in constriction vanishes. You can relax and let go. You are being guided by the Source within yourself, to count your blessings, to "get it" that your life is more blessed than you ever thought. In midlife, you have many stories to tell – so write them, and let us, your readers read them!

The best way to keep your passion alive is to make your number one relationship in the world be that between you and your Source of being.
Wayne Dyer [87]

Writing this book has lifted me up and deepened my trust in my Writer Within. I thank you for reading and for joining a community of writers who know that writing can be a sacred act; that partnering with your Writer Within will change you.

When you choose to love and marry your Self – self and Self become one, if you let them. This relationship with your Creative Self, your Writer Within, is for life. And if you treat her as well as, even better than your neighbor or your lover, your creativity will thrive – and so will you.

When you draw forth what is within you, rather than expecting others to fix you, you contribute in a fundamental way to peace on this planet. When you encourage your Creative Self to emerge, your life force expands, fosters peaceful relations, and shines your bright light into our world.

When you write, the guardians of your soul whisper their names,

Bow before you like elders in a sacred ceremony, chanting Namaste,

So, you offer your thoughts up to the divine, and indeed remember

Deep inside you, buried so deep you often can't find it,

Deep inside is a spark, and by blowing it onto the page, it ignites

and illuminates your own Greatness.

The End

Notes

1. Diana Vilas, "The spiritual potential of menopause," in *Our Turn, Our Time*, edited by Cynthia Black (Hillsboro Oregon: Beyond Words Publishing, Inc., 2000), 234.
2. Ibid., 238.
3. Daniel Amen, *Making a Good Brain Great* (New York: Three Rivers Press, 2005), 178.
4. Ibid., xii.
5. Janice Brewi and Anne Brennan, *Mid-Life: psychological and Spiritual Perspectives* (New York: The CrossRoad Publishing Company, 1987), 89.
6. Dr. Gene D. Cohen, M.D., Ph.D., *The Creative Age: Awakening Human Potential in the Second Half of Life* (New York: Quill, an Imprint of HarperCollins Publishers, 2000), 78.
7. Sir Ken Robinson and Lou Aronica, *The Element: How finding your passion changes everything* (London: Penguin Books Ltd., 2009), 56.
8. J. Rumi, "Feeling the Shoulder of the Lion," Trans by Coleman Barks (Internet: Allspirit Poetry: Selections from the poetry of Rumi, Mathnawi, III), 4391-4472.
9. Robinson and Aronica, *The Element*, 56.
10. Rainer Maria Rilke, *Letters to a Young Poet* (New York: W. W. Norton & Company, 1993), 18-19.
11. Julia Cameron, *The Artist's Way: a Spiritual Path to Higher Creativity* (New York: Jeremy P. Tarcher/Perigee Books, 1992), 82.
12. May Sarton, *Journal of a Solitude: The intimate diary of a year in the life of a creative woman* (New York: W.W. Norton & Co., 1977), 11.
13. Wayne W. Dyer, *Excuses Begone!* (California: Hay House, Inc., 2009), 124.
14. Lia Cardarelli, "Nobelmen: neuroscientists discover cerebral hemisphere brain functions," *The Varsity.ca/articles/29668* (Toronto: May 29, 2010), Science.
15. Alex Osborne, *Applied Imagination* (New York: Charles Scribner's Sons, 1963), 15.
16. Sidney Parnes, "Effects of extended effort in creative problem-solving," *Journal of Educational Psychology* (52, 1961), 121.
17. Graham Wallas, *The Art of Thought* (New York: Harcourt Brace, 1926), 51.
18. Deena Metzger, *Writing for Your Life* (San Francisco: Harper, 1992), 56.
19. Rollo May, *The Courage to Create* (New York: Bantam Books with W.W. Norton & Co, Inc., 1976), 64.
20. Sarton, *Journal of a Solitude*,195.
21. Clark E. Moustakas, *Creativity and Conformity* (New York: D. Van Nostrand Company, 1967), 8.
22. Cohen, *The Creative Age*,12.
23. Rollo May, *The Meaning of Anxiety, rev edition* (New York: W.W. Norton & Co., 1977), 377.
24. May, *The Courage to Create*, 4.
25. Carl Jung, in Marshall Paule, *Praisesong for the Widow* (New York: Dutton, 1984), 83.
26. Kathleen A. Brehony, *Awakening at Midlife: A Guide to Reviving your Spirit, Recreating Your Life, and Returning to Your Truest Self* (New York: Riverhead Books,1996), 13.
27. James Hollis, Ph.D., *Finding Meaning in the Second Half of Life: how to finally really grow up* (New York: Gotham Books, Penguin Group (USS) Inc., 2005), 12.
28. Sarton, *Journal of a Solitude*, 40.

Notes

29. James Hollis, Ph.D., *Finding Meaning in the Second Half of Life: how to finally really grow up* (New York: Gotham Books, Penguin Group (USS) Inc., 2005), 12.
30. Wayne W. Dyer, *Excuses Begone! How to change lifelong, self-defeating thinking habits* (California: Hay House, Inc., 2009), 123.
31. Langston Hughes, "Dreams," *The Collected Poems of Langston Hughes* (New York: Alfred A. Knopf/Vintage, 1994).
32. Jack Canfield, In a teleseminar interview with Steve Harrison (Broomall PA: Bradley Communications Corp., Oct 15, 2008).
33. Ibid.
34. Barbara Sher, *It's only too late If You Don't Start Now: How to Create Your Second Life at Any Age* (New York: Dell Publishing, a divison of Random House, Inc., 1998), 164-165.
35. Ibid. 165.
36. Dr. Whitehall and Dr. Umbach, *Webster's New World Dictionary* (New York:College Edition, 1965), 71.
37. Dan Poynter, *Books That Were Originally Self-Published* (Santa Barbara, Ca: Para Publishing, www.parapublishing.com/files, Document 155), 1-4.
38. Cohen, *The Creative Age*, 17.
39. May Sarton, *The House By The Sea: a journal* (New York: W.W. Norton & Company, 1981), 188.
40. Wayne Dyer, *Excuses Begone!*, 123.
41. Gary Zukav, *The Seat of The Soul* (A Fireside book, published by Simon & Schuster Inc., 1990), 60-61.
42. Brewi and Brennan, *Mid-Life: psychological and Spiritual Perspectives*, 136.
43. Ibid., 105.
44. Annette Moser-Wellman, *The Five Faces of Genius* (New York: Penguin Books, 2002), 148.
45. Clarissa Pinkola Estes, *Women Who Run with the Wolves: Myths and Stories of the Wild Woman Archetype* (New York: Ballantine Books, 1992), 301.
46. Metzger, *Writing for your Life*, 17.
47. Foundation for Inner Peace, *A Course in Miracles, Volume 2, Workbook* (New York: Foundation for Inner Peace, 1981), 210.
48. Foundation for Inner Peace, *A Course in Miracles, Volume 1, Text* (New York: Foundation for Inner Peace, 1981), 593.
49. *A Course in Miracles*, Workbook, 214.
50. Sher, *It's Only Too Late if You Don't Start Now*, 264.
51. Ibid, 188.
52. Ibid, 188.
53. Dr.Wayne W. Dyer, *The Power of Intention: Learning to Co-create Your World Your Way* (Carlsbad, Ca: Hay House, Inc., 2004), 6.
54. Brewi and Brennan, *Mid-Life: psychological and Spiritual Perspectives*, 138.
55. Jean Shinda Bolen, *Urgent Message from MOTHER: Gather the Women, Save the WORLD* (San Francisco: Conari Press, 2005), 159.
56. Gabriel Lusser Rico, *Writing The Natural Way: Using Right-Brain Techniques to Release Your Expressive Powers* (Los Angeles: J.P.Tarcher, Inc., 1983), 82.
57. Connie Goldman and Richard Mahler, *Secrets of becoming a Late Bloomer* (Center City, Minnesota: Hazelden, 1995), 247-248.

Notes

58. Tristine Rainer, *Your Life as Story: Discovering the "New Autobiography" and Writing Memoir as Literature* (New York: Jeremy P. Tarcher/Putnam, 1998), 37.
59. Frederick Franck, *The Zen of Seeing: Seeing/Drawing as Meditation* (New York: Vintage Books, A Division of Random House, 1973), 6.
60. Osborn, Alex, *Applied Imagination: Principles and Procedures of Creative Problem-Solving* (N.Y.: Charles Scribner's Sons. 1953), 6.
61. Ibid., 7.
62. Sidney Parnes, YouTube, August 5, 2010.
63. Osborn, *Applied Imagination*, 18.
64. Melba Burns, *"A comparison of three creative problem solving methodologies:" A Dissertation* (Denver: U. of Denver Pub, 1983).
65. Jan Phillips, *Marry Your Muse: Making a Lasting Commitment to your Creativity* (Wheaton, Illinois: Quest Books, Theosophical Publishing House, 1997), 7.
66. Johann Wolfgang von Goethe, *Classic Quotes, Quotation #39959* (www.quotationspage.com).
67. William Hutchinson Murray, *The Scottish Expedition* (London: J. M. Dent & Sons Publishers, 1951), 2.
68. Wayne Dyer, *Excuses Begone!* 129
69. Annette Moser-Wellman, *The Five Faces of Genius* (New York: Penguin Books, 2002), 189.
70. Joan Lemieux, "Women Navigators" in *Our Turn, Our Time*, edited by Cynthia Black (Hillsboro Oregon: Beyond Words Publishing, Inc., 2000), 143.
71. Sandra H. Martz, *When I am an old woman I shall wear purple* (New York: Papier-Mache Press, 1991), 1.
72. Clarissa Pinkola Estees, *Women Who Run With The Wolves*, 317-318.
73. Jalal al-Din Rumi, *Allspirit Poety*, "Selections from the poetry of Rumi," Translated by Coleman Barks, Ode 2865, Internet.
74. Shinoda Bolen, *Urgent Message from MOTHER*, 76.
75. Cohen, *The Creative Age*, 85.
76. Anthony Robbins, *Awaken the Giant Within: How to Take Immediate Control of Your Mental, Emotional, Physical and Financial Destiny!* (New York: Free Press, A Division of Simon & Schuster, Inc., 1991), 285.
77. Amen, *Making a Good Brain Great*,175.
78. Ibid., 175.
79. IMDb "Biography for Barbara Cartland," *Barbara Cartland - Biography* (The Internet Movie Database, 2010), 1.
80. Diane Vilas, "The Spiritual Potential of Menopause," in *Our Turn, Our Time*, 240.
81. Shinoda Bolen, *Urgent Message from MOTHER*, 162
82. Ibid., 157.
83. Ibid., 158.
84. *A Course in Miracles, Workbook*, 216.
85. Robert MacNeil, *Wordstruck: a Memoir* (New York: Viking Penguin Inc., 1989), 216.
86. James Hollis, *Finding Meaning in the Second Half of Life*, 158.
87. Wayne Dyer, *Excuses Begone!*, 126.

All unreferenced poems are by the author, Melba Burns.

Acknowledgements

I acknowledge you, my students, past and present, for you have inspired many of the ideas in this book. You have kept me reaching for more motivational exercises so we can all move forward in our writing – and you keep me on my toes. I admire and respect all of you wonderful people who have gone beyond your fears regarding creativity, faced them courageously, and have written amazing pieces. I am so grateful to you and have felt privileged to witness your moments of awe as you have read out a new story or poem – in wonder that you actually wrote it. You have truly dived in to your long-lost or forgotten creativity and honored it with your passion, as well as your discipline to writing. I love you all, and am forever grateful to you for giving your best Self to each of us in the group. You courageous people, some who have been writing for years, some of you just beginning, and other brand new writers – you are why I wrote this book. Thank you so much for your trust in me.

I am also grateful to friends who have gently nudged me and asked the crucial question: "How's the book coming?" and "When can I read a copy?" Some of these are June Swadron, Karyn Mathison, Ervin Atchison, Frances Allden, Brenda Dineen, Isabelle Baillie, Jena Kros, and others, who listened patiently to my frustrations with kind words of encouragement.

Acknowledgements

I acknowledge a serious debt of gratitude to my dear friend Deb Cameron Fawkes, who gifted me with hours and hours of her time; editing, supporting and encouraging me, and without whom this book would not be in the publishable form it is now. Thank you so much my friend.

Gratitude to Fred Cogswell, a dear mentor and friend, who published my first book of poetry, In The Inbetween, and who believed in me, long before I did myself; the memory of his sweet encouragement led me through.

Thanks to all the people who took time out of their lives to read the book and give me glowing testimonials.

I appreciate all the love I receive from the spiritual community in Vancouver, and the prayers which have truly helped me in the completion of this book.

Thanks to Eve Lees who created a beautiful cover, in such a short span of time – for we do judge a book by the cover.

Much gratitude goes to Roxane Leigh, who did a superb job on the interior design of the book.

I am grateful to all of you who believe in, support and encourage creativity, and I do hope that you enjoy, and learn from this book.

Sincerely,

Melba Burns

For further information:
To order more books, to inquire about writing workshops
speaking engagements, or teleseminars,
please write to Melba Burns at melbawrites@gmail.com.
Or visit the website, www.melbaburns.com.

No matter what you do, please keep on writing!

Manufactured by Amazon.ca
Acheson, AB